THE
CALL
of the
SEA

*A visual timeline of Sunderland's shipbuilding
history through to the Tall Ships Race of 2018*

Written and illustrated by
Naomi A Austin

Foreword by
Architect and TV Presenter
George Clarke

This book is dedicated to
my Mum and Dad, Alix & Keith who have always
believed in me; and to my Godparents
Jan and Mel McQuillin who always supported
me and who are missed every day.

Published by UK Book Publishing – ukbookpublishing.com
Printed in the EU by Print Trail – printtrail.com

ISBN: 978-1-912183-49-4

CONTENTS

FOREWORD

Some say the beating heart of Sunderland was football or coal mining. Of course, these were both incredibly important to the entire North-East; football still is. But, Wearside came into existence because of its beautiful river and the banks of the river then grew into one of the most influential industrial towns in the world because of something bigger than football or coal mining - shipbuilding. This wonderful industry began in Wearmouth as far back as the 14th century, hundreds of years before the first football was kicked or the first lump of coal was mined. Shipbuilding was the beating heart of Sunderland.

1346 was the year Thomas Menville had his shipbuilding yard in Hendon, just South of Wearmouth, and it was in Hendon in the early 1980's I'd hang out with my Grandad at weekends and on school holidays to work on his fishing trawler, the 'Mary Anne'. I'll never forget those days. Turning up at the docks in my Grandad's Leyland CF van and seeing his red trawler sitting in the water always made me so proud of him. He'd never built a boat before, yet he was brave enough to build her from scratch to become a Captain of his own small vessel and take her out to the North Sea to earn his crust as a prawn fisherman.

I knew, even at such a young age, as I played in the docks and messed around on his boat that I was treading over the footsteps of tens of thousands of great men who, over a period of 600 years, had turned Sunderland into one of the greatest shipbuilding towns in the world. The smell of the sea, the salty air, the fishing nets, the grease, diesel and rusting metal and even the sweat of those working around us made me love being on that boat and around the people who worked in the docks.

Of course, my grandad's humble trawler cannot be compared to the likes of the breathtaking scale and engineering wonder of the 'Naess Crusader' (1973) or the elegance and beauty of the clipper ship Torrens (1877) that set sail from the River Wear. But, in my world, in its own small way, the 'Mary-Anne' reflected the grit, determination and blood, sweat and tears that went into every vessel that was built in my hometown.

December 21st 1972:
The Naess Crusader under tow to the fitting out yard at Manor
Quay by the tugs Marsden, Prestwick and Westsider.
The tugs to the right of the picture are the Whitburn and Cornhill.
(TWAM ref. DT.TUR/2/60988A)

5

The people of Sunderland are known as 'Mackems' for good reason. It stems from the phrase "we mack'em and they tack'em" (we make them and they take them). The expression dates back to the height of Sunderland's shipbuilding industry and its meaning has been interpreted in many different ways over the years, but what cannot be disputed is that with this nickname, the people of Sunderland regarded themselves as a town of 'makers'. Makers of incredible ships. In 1815 there were 600 ships being built along the River Wear in no less that 31 yards. We were 'makers' of ships that changed the world. We should always be proud of that.

Unfortunately, after World War II a large number of yards began to close and the industry fell into decline. The heartbeat began to slow.

In 1984, when I was 10 years old, there were still nearly 5000 people employed in Sunderland's shipyards. But 4 years later on the 7th December 1988 the last remaining yard closed. I remember shedding a tear that day. Not long afterwards my Grandad sold his trawler.

I understand that industries come and go and in a globalised world there is fierce competition to build ships cheaper. But we were good; very good. Some say the best ship builders in the world. When 71% of the earth's surface is water and there is so much demand for goods to be transported on a mass scale across our oceans and seas, I still don't fully understand how we let such a beautiful industry die.

Shipbuilding has now gone from my home town. Its industrial heart has stopped beating. But, Naomi Austin has put together the most wonderful book to keep the memories of those thriving industrial days alive. Combined with her elegant drawings she captures the stories of those ships that changed the world as well as celebrating the lives of the incredible people who built them.

The people of Sunderland are some of the most passionate and proud people you are ever likely to meet and they will continue to feel that pride with every single page turn of this book. I know I did and I can't thank Naomi enough for writing it...and if my Grandad were still alive today, he would thank her too!

Architect and TV Presenter
George Clarke

INTRODUCTION

In 1993, I was incredibly fortunate to be chosen as one of 12 young trainees to sail in the Tall Ships Race from Newcastle to Bergen, Norway, representing the North East of England. Despite having never sailed before - the closest I'd come to sailing was my Auntie's mirror dinghy on Semerwater in North Yorkshire - and with no prior experience of ships, I had a real love for the water… but it had never occurred to me there was something like the Tall Ships Race! Nevertheless, three weeks spent on the Sir Winston Churchill saw the beginning of a passion for everything to do with tall ships, and over the past 25 years I have followed these ships and their adventures with great interest.

I wanted to get close to them whenever they were in the North East of England - Newcastle in 2005, then Hartlepool in 2010, where I signed up as a Ship Liaison Officer looking after the crew and trainees, sharing my experience with the younger sailors. The Tall Ships Regatta then came to Blyth in 2016 and I was lucky enough to be a Ship Liaison Officer once more, this time for the Polish Dar Młodzieży, the biggest ship in the race.

My involvement with the Tall Ships Race over the years has given me a real pride in the role and made me realise how much I wanted to get back on the water to experience another maritime adventure. Just before the Blyth Regatta, it was announced Sunderland had been chosen as host port for the 2018 race and I didn't hesitate in putting my name forward once more. It was then the realisation dawned - when the ships arrive in Sunderland it would be 25 years since I sailed on the Sir Winston Churchill. The decision was taken to create something which would celebrate this anniversary alongside the visit of the Tall Ships to Sunderland, for the first time in its history.

The initial intention was to create an exhibition of my drawings of some of these ships but after delving deeper into the history of Sunderland and its shipbuilding heritage, I started to realise it was going to become a much bigger project and from that came this book.

It is at this juncture I should point something out - I'm a born and bred Geordie who never had much reason to go to Sunderland. Growing up, it was "just a place south of the river", albeit well-known due to the football rivalry, but I can honestly say I never visited the city as a child given I had everything I needed in Newcastle. However, this situation was going to change.

In 2014, I started work at Sunderland University and through this I finally became acquainted with the city. I quickly became aware that Sunderland, only 12 miles away from where I grew up, was a vibrant, colourful place with locals just as friendly as those from Newcastle. It's a well-known fact that people from the North East are friendly anyway, but I started to get a sense of the real loyalty of the 'Mackems'.

There have been shipyards on both the River Wear and River Tyne, but I then discovered Sunderland was the biggest shipbuilding town in the World at one point in history. It was time Sunderland's shipbuilding heritage came out from the shadow of Newcastle, hence the desire to produce this book was cemented in my mind. The good people of Sunderland deserved something to remind them of this amazing shipbuilding heritage, to re-instil pride in their history as we welcome the millions of visitors to the Wear for the Tall Ships Race in 2018.

Whilst conducting this research, I have met some fascinating people and heard amazing tales of the shipbuilding industry on the River Wear. There are so many stunning photographs of ships being built and the people who made this their livelihood, but a lot of these images are now hidden away in archives. This book, with its stories and illustrations, will hopefully ensure the tales of these workers of the River Wear, many of whom are now in their 70s and 80s, can be shared with a new generation instead of being lost forever.

Ultimately, this research is a celebration of Sunderland's maritime heritage and revival, from the first ships built on the Wear in the 1880s through to the 2018 Tall Ships Race when, once again, the Wear will be teeming with maritime activity. I do hope this book will be of interest to both young and old, encouraging people to once again talk about a history of which they should be incredibly proud, as well as generating excitement in welcoming the Tall Ships and hundreds of different nations to the region. I also hope my experiences and memories of being a first-time sail trainee will inspire more young people to take part in a Tall Ships adventure.

By doing this research, I've developed a deep-rooted respect for the people of Sunderland and how much they have to offer. I will always be a loyal Geordie, but now feel very much part of a far bigger community and am so proud to say I'm from the North East of England.

On a final note, the Call of the Sea has proved to be too strong yet again; in July 2018 I will be joining the Alexander Von Humboldt II as a sail trainee racing to Esjberg, Denmark, on the first leg of the race and then the 'Cruise in Company' from Esjberg to Stavanger in Norway on the Statsraad Lehmkuhl. Here's hoping the sea legs are just as strong 25 years after I first raced a tall ship across the North Sea!

Naomi A Austin

Aerial view of the River Wear showing 'Naess Crusader' nearing completion at the fitting out quay June 1973. (TWAM ref. DT.TUR/2/61775B).

These photographs were taken by the Newcastle based firm Turners (Photography) Ltd. They celebrate the construction of the OBO (oil/bulk/ore) carrier 'Naess Crusader, covering the early stages in January 1972 through her launch on 21 December 1972 to her completion and sea trials in July 1973.

1: SHIPBUILDING ON THE WEAR

If the art of...

SHIP BUILDING

...were in the wood, ships would exist by...

NATURE

- Aristotle

Joseph L. Thompson & Sons Shipyard
original photograph featured in the
publicity campaign 'The Art of Shipbuilding'
published in 1946 to promote the firms of
Joseph L. Thompson & Sons and
Sir James Laing & Sons Ltd.

'Sunderland - The Greatest Shipbuilding Town in the World'

Sunderland city centre as we know it today was initially called Bishopwearmouth; the actual locality of Sunderland was closer to the mouth of the River Wear, although still on the south banks. This is now known as the East End, or Old Sunderland, and is where the most bustling parts of the town could be found from the 1200s.

Although Sunderland first became known as a coal port, in 1346 its fortunes were to change when Thomas Menville became the first recorded shipbuilder at Hendon. Fast forward four centuries and by 1790 around nineteen ships per year were being built here with rapid expansion soon to make its mark on the town. By 1814 there were three shipyards building 31 ships per year but just one year later, Sunderland was the thriving home to 31 working shipyards, four dry docks, four floating docks and five boat-builders' yards with over 600 ships being built each year.

Sunderland soon lay claim to the title of 'Biggest Shipbuilding Town in the World'; in 1840 the town had an impressive 76 shipyards with a third of the ships built in the UK between 1846 and 1854 from Wearside. In 1850 alone, over 150 wooden vessels were built on the Wear by 2,025 shipwrights with a further 2,000 people being employed in related industries. Moving with the times, Sunderland first began building iron ships in 1852 and 23 years later wooden shipbuilding was to cease.

World War I saw a period of unemployment in the shipbuilding industry and only two ships were launched in 1932. Nevertheless, World War II saw a revived demand for new ships. By 1942, the town reached its highest production level with 1.5 million tonnes of merchant shipping built, some 27% of the total output of British yards during the wartime.

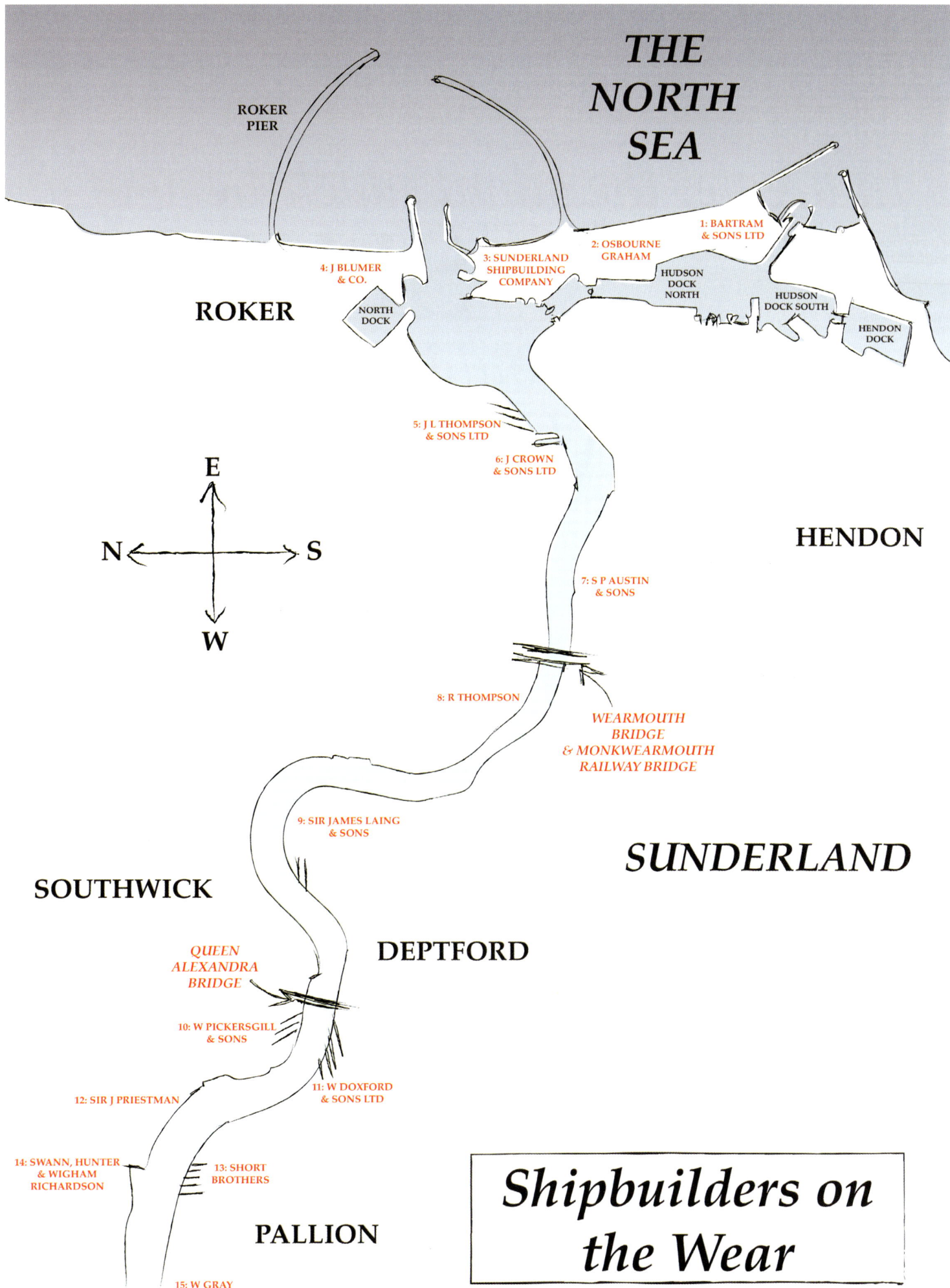

THE NORTH SEA

ROKER PIER

4: J BLUMER & CO.

ROKER

NORTH DOCK

3: SUNDERLAND SHIPBUILDING COMPANY

2: OSBOURNE GRAHAM

1: BARTRAM & SONS LTD

HUDSON DOCK NORTH

HUDSON DOCK SOUTH

HENDON DOCK

5: J L THOMPSON & SONS LTD

6: J CROWN & SONS LTD

HENDON

7: S P AUSTIN & SONS

E

N ← → S

W

8: R THOMPSON

WEARMOUTH BRIDGE & MONKWEARMOUTH RAILWAY BRIDGE

9: SIR JAMES LAING & SONS

SUNDERLAND

SOUTHWICK

QUEEN ALEXANDRA BRIDGE

DEPTFORD

10: W PICKERSGILL & SONS

11: W DOXFORD & SONS LTD

12: SIR J PRIESTMAN

14: SWANN, HUNTER & WIGHAM RICHARDSON

13: SHORT BROTHERS

PALLION

15: W GRAY

Shipbuilders on the Wear

In a gale, the silent machinery of a...

SHIP

...would catch not only the...

POWER

...but the...

WILD

...and exulting voice of the World's...

SOUL

- Joseph Conrad
'The Mirror of the Sea'

So, Sunderland retained this notable title for many years, although some have tried to dispute this given the River Clyde produced 286,420 tonnes of ship in 1938 compared to the 169,001 tonnes produced on the River Wear. However, as stated in Smith and Holden's 'Where Ships Are Born' (1946), the River Clyde's shipyards and production were spread across a number of locations along the banks of the Clyde, whereas the ships built in Sunderland were all concentrated in the one town.

Throughout the 1950s and 1960s, Sunderland continued to lead the way but the town started to see the closure or mergers of more and more shipyards as global shipping production increased making it difficult for British shipyards to compete on the global stage. The demise of the industry began in 1977 with the nationalisation of British shipbuilding and by 1980 the last two remaining Wearside shipyards merged. From a thriving industry only half a decade ago, some 4300 people were employed in the shipyards by 1984; four years later, Doxford's, the last remaining shipyard on the Wear closed, bringing the long and prestigious history of shipbuilding on the Wear to an end on 7th December 1988.

Throughout its history, Sunderland had over 400 registered shipyards with thousands upon thousands of men and women working together. Shipbuilding may no longer exist on the River Wear but the legacy is still visible throughout the city. Sunderland might have once been given the title of 'Largest Shipbuilding Town in the World' but to many it will always be the 'Greatest Shipbuilding Town in the World.'

April 1860
Launch of the barque 'Vencedora' built by Robert
Thompson & Sons, North Sands.

Vessel type: Copper ore trader

28 July 1961
View of the cargo ship 'Eastern Rover' ready for launch, taken through the shell plates of her sister ship 'Eastern Ranger' built by J.L. Thompson & Sons Ltd, North Sands, Sunderland. (TWAM ref. DS.JLT/4/PH/1/706/2/2).

Vessel type: General Cargo
Length: 404ft

It's all we're...

SKILLED

...in, we will be...

SHIPBUILDING

- Elvis Costello

4 June 1954
Knocking out the chocks before the launch of the tanker 'Andwi',
built by John Crown & Sons Ltd.

Vessel type: Oil Tanker
Length: 548ft 6in

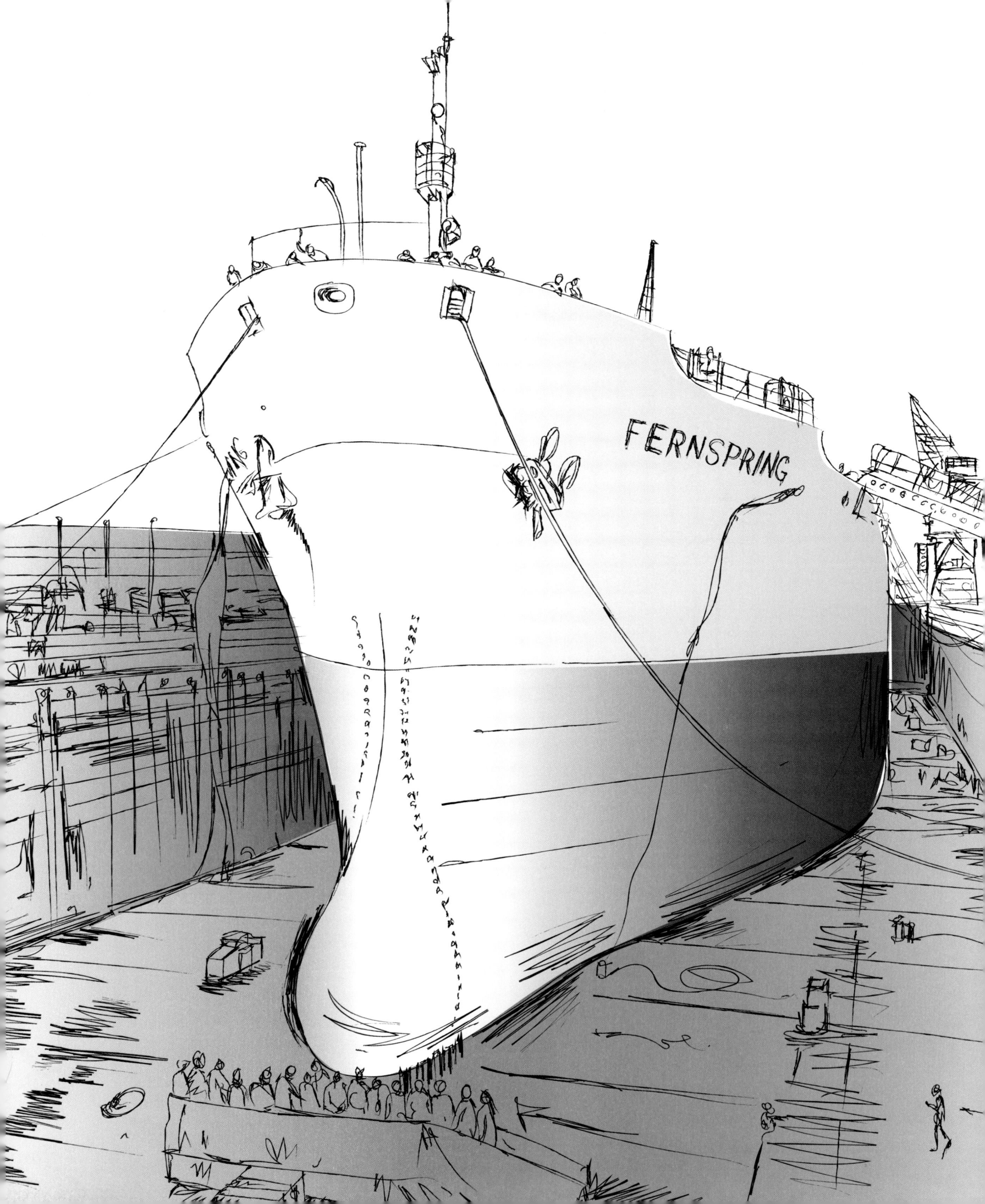

May 1967
The naming ceremony of the Fernspring.
She was launched at the North Sands shipyard, Sunderland,
on December 30th 1966.

Vessel type: Bulk carrier
Length: 708ft 6in

26 May 1959
Aerial view of the North Sands
shipyard of J.L. Thompson & Sons,
Sunderland. The image appears to show the
shipyard's new pre-fabrication shed under
construction. Work is also underway on a new
slipway.

(TWAM ref. DT.TUR/2/22169B).

11 March 1959
The cargo ship 'Miss Chandris' ready for launch at the shipyard
of William Doxford & Sons, Pallion.

Vessel type: General cargo
Length: 509ft 2 in

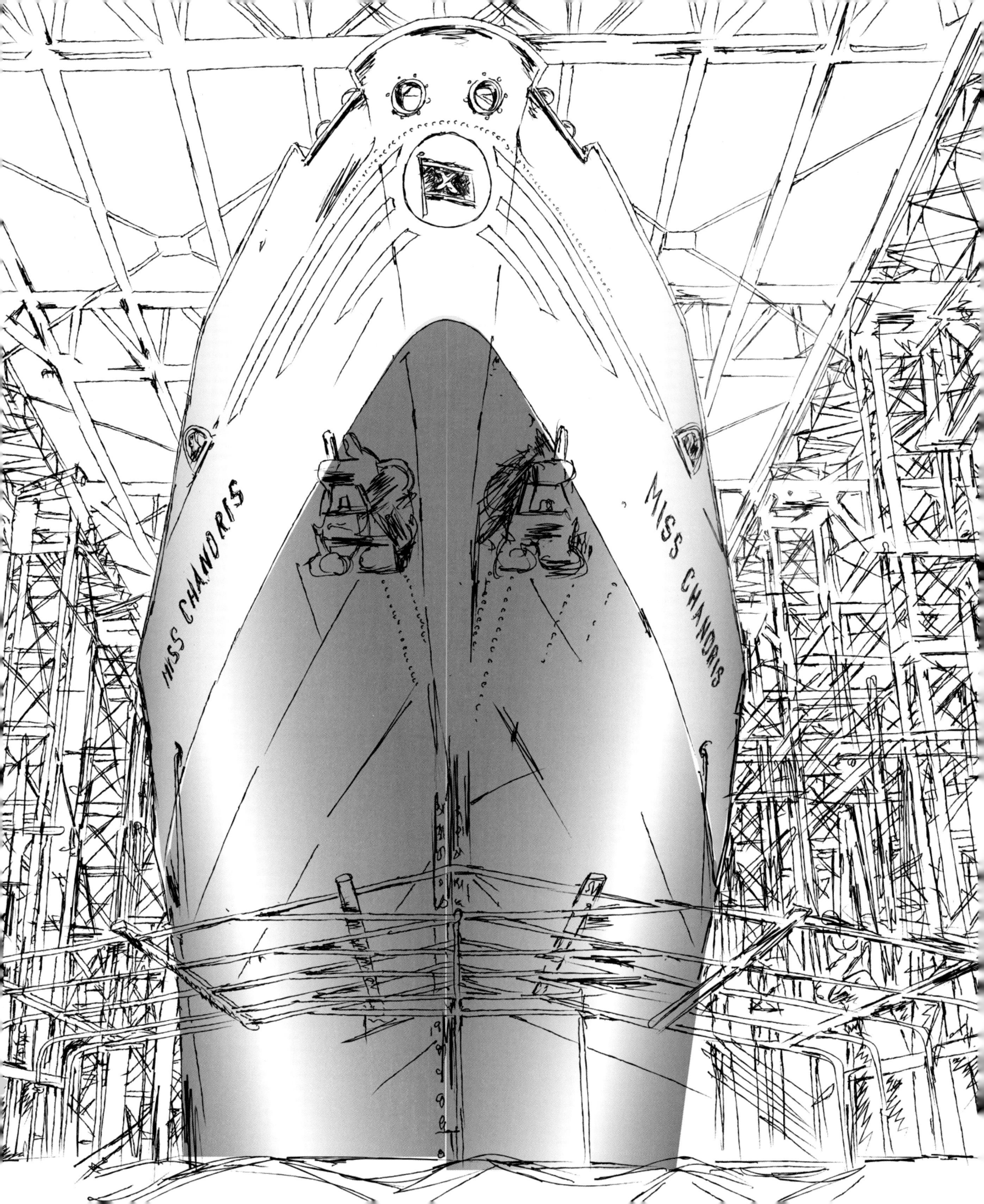

Pallion, 11 March 1959
The young girl in the picture is Eugenia Chandris, daughter of the Greek
shipowner Dimitris Chandris, ready to launch the cargo ship 'Miss Chandris',
built by William Doxford & Sons. At 20 months old
she was believed to be the youngest person to launch a ship in
Sunderland.

(TWAM ref. DS.DOX/4/PH/1/830/1/3).

I am not afraid of...
STORMS
...for I am learning how to...
SAIL
...my ship.

- Louisa May Alcott

24 September 1957
The cargo ship 'Harpagus' being towed to the fitting out quay after launch by William Doxford & Sons Ltd. On the left is the cargo ship 'Errington Court' being fitted out at the Southwick Yard of Austin & Pickersgill Ltd. and on the right, the 'Dona Katerina' built by Doxfords.

October 1959
Deck view on the tanker 'Aluco'.
She was launched at the North
Sands shipyard of
J.L. Thompson & Sons,
Sunderland on 23 April 1959.

Vessel type: Oil tanker
Length: 559ft 11in

11 February 1941
A sponsor preparing to launch the tanker 'Empire Coral'
built by Sir James Laing & Sons Ltd, Sunderland.

Vessel type: Oil tanker
Length: 493ft 8in

8 December 1965
The tanker 'Daphnella' under tow on the River Wear
after launch at the North Sands shipyard of J.L. Thompson & Sons, Sunderland.

(TWAM ref. DS.JLT/4/PH/1/716/2/3).

Vessel type: Oil tanker
Length: 799ft 7in

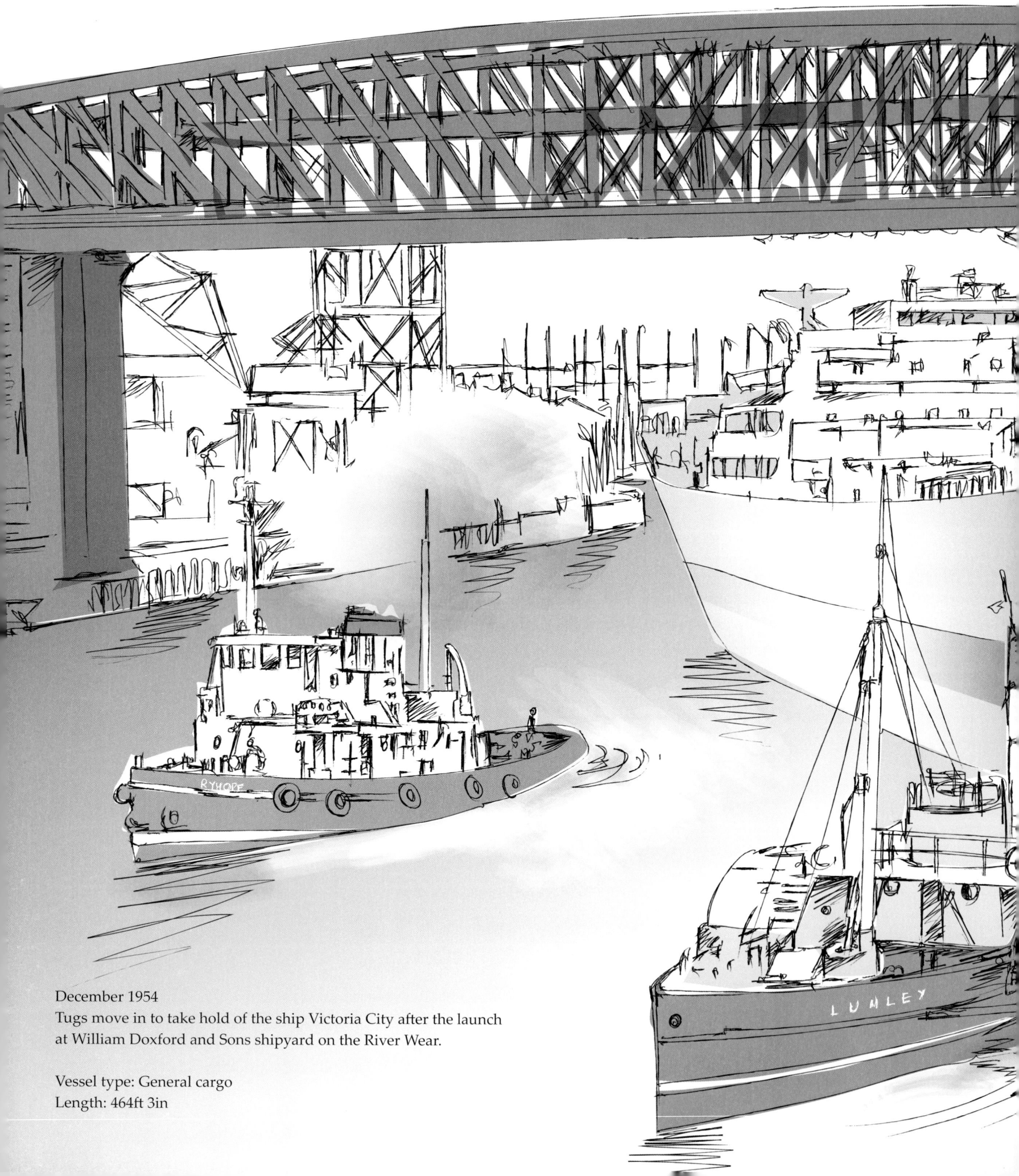

December 1954
Tugs move in to take hold of the ship Victoria City after the launch
at William Doxford and Sons shipyard on the River Wear.

Vessel type: General cargo
Length: 464ft 3in

VICTORIA CITY

November 13th 1967
The stern frame being manoeuvred into position on the first SD14 to be completed by Austin & Pickersgill Shipyard, the 'Nicola'. The 'Nicola' was the first in a long line of standard ships designed by the Sunderland shipyard.
Construction started October 1967, completed February 1968. The SD14 (Shelter Deck 14,000 tons deadweight.) was designed to replace the surviving Liberty ships built by American yards during the Second World War.

Vessel type: Bulk carrier
Length: 708ft 6in

A ship in...

HARBOUR

...is safe, but that is not what...

SHIPS

...are built for.

- John A. Shedd

29 December 1967
View of the first SD14 'Nicola' as she is launched at the
Southwick shipyard of Austin & Pickersgill, Sunderland.

(TWAM ref. DT.TUR/4/AG3684C)

October 22nd 1957
View of the tanker Spinanger being moored
after launch from the North Sands shipyard
of J. L. Thompson & Sons. The launch of
Spinanger was unusual in that it was carried
out without the assistance
of tugboats. This was due to industrial
action by the Wear tugboatmen.

Vessel type: Oil tanker
Length: 559ft 8in

CEo. CLA

April 1949
Aerial view of shipyards on the River Wear.
The shipyard of William Doxford & Sons is on the
centre left of the picture, while William Pickersgill &
Sons is on the right. The majority of slipways on the
river were built at an angle or diagonal, this was
because the Wear was too narrow to allow a
conventional launch of a large vessel.

(TWAM ref. DT.TUR/2/2829C).

49

"I left school at Christmas 1943 and started work in J.L Thompson's time office on 3rd January 1944. This was a large dome shaped corrugated sheet structure at the bottom of Zetland Street in the middle of the road opposite the North Sands gate. It was a temporary set up while the original office was rebuilt after being destroyed by German bombs.

The time office consisted of Mr. Boreham the manager, and Mr. Thurlbeck; Mr. Hartford; Mr. Beryl, Mr. Vietch and Mr. Todd all who wrote out the time sheets before I was given the job of walking up to Laing's shipyard office with them to work out the wages until our new offices were built. We also had Mrs. Gowdy who did the paperwork for the National Savings certificates to be taken out of the men's wages.

I used to stamp the number of every man on the time boards which were made out of light cardboard; about 4 inches by 3 inches, and the men drew them at 7.30 every morning and wrote the number of the ship they were working on and handed them in at finishing time each day. I also used to hand out the boards from 7 o' clock each morning with other office staff.

After 2 to 3 months we moved into the new completed office block and one of my jobs was walking around the shipyard (with no safety helmets) to hand out what were called peace books as some men were on 'peace' (bonus).

During each day various foremen came into the office; some wearing bowler hats, and I got to know them quite well. As I was approaching my 16th birthday Mr. Boreham, my time office manager, asked if I fancied serving my time as a joiner and I jumped at the chance as I'd always liked woodwork. I'd enjoyed working in the office and it gave me a good experience.

I started down the Manor Quay joiners shop and my first job was making cans of tea. I had to go on the ship at 7.30am and collect all the joiner's cans and make their tea then take them back at 9 o' clock for their break. I had to do the same for their 12 o' clock dinner hour.

After a few weeks I was put on a bench to learn joiner work. I had to make a tool box and get a £2 and 10 shilling tool order to take to Brumwell's on the High Street which was taken out of my wages at 2 shillings per week! I think my weekly wage was about 16 shillings and 6 pence, when I paid off the tool order they would give me another order and this went on until you had all your required tools.

I worked on various benches with older joiners making doors and ships furniture and working on the ship learning how to mark off accommodation and how to construct it in noisy, and sometimes dangerous, conditions from the welder's flashes and burner's sparks.

We all had to do National Service at 18 but if you were serving an apprenticeship you were able to defer until you were 21 and you had finished your time. I was 21 on 6th September 1950 and the following day I was on my way to Wrexham in North Wales to join the Army for 2 years National Service.

When I was demobbed in 1952 with 3 stripes as a Sergeant, J.L. Thompson's had to give me 6 months work as instructed by the Government. When there was no finishing work for joiners I was paid off and did the rounds whenever there was work. I worked at Bartrams, Austins, Pickersgills, Doxfords and Shorts as well as construction sites in the North East. I also had to do 3 years in the Army emergency Reserve after I was demobbed, which meant I had to go to Ruabon in North Wales for 2 weeks training every year for a period of 3 years.

I worked on a lot of Wear built ships, and one that stands out is the Silverbriar built by J.L. Thompson's. I think it was the best looking ship to be built on the Wear. It had two funnels; the front one was false and housed the Captain's accommodation with a link into the wheelhouse.

I retired when I turned 65 in September 1994 as a site agent. All the experience I had in the yards and on the construction sites was memorable as I crept up the ladder from being a joiner to a site agent."

Alf Redford
Former Shipyard worker

51

My heart is stirred when the winds blow...

FREE

...and the...

SHIPS

...go out on the ebbing tide

-Roselle Mercier Montgomery

Early 1950's
Austin shipyard workers walking up
Pann Lane at the end of their shift.
In the background is J.L. Thompson's
yard with ships being fitted out.

29 August 1972
Work nearing completion at the North Sands
shipyard, Sunderland, on the stern of the OBO carrier
'Naess Crusader'
Builder: Sunderland Shipbuilders Ltd.
North Sands, Sunderland

Vessel Type: Oil/Bulk/Ore Carrier
Length: 957ft 6in

'A Beast of a Ship'

The Naess Crusader and her sister ship, the Nordic Chieftain, were the largest ships ever to be built on the River Wear. Commissioned by Anglo-Eastern Bulkships Ltd., the Naess Crusader was the first to be built with work starting on her in January 1972 by Sunderland Shipbuilders Limited at the North Sands Yard.

She was to carry iron ore, oil and bulk cargoes and was launched on the 21st December 1972 on a dark, dreary, misty afternoon. Regardless of the weather, her launch drew a large crowd of people fascinated by this incredible feat of engineering. She was then towed to Manor Quay to be fitted out, finally being completed in July 1973, weighing in at 158,000 tonnes and measuring over 950ft in length. Her cargo capacity was 172,880 cubic metres, the equivalent of having nearly 70 Olympic sized swimming pools on board.

The Naess Crusader went through a number of name changes and owners throughout her life before finally being decommissioned in 1998 and broken up in Bangladesh.

In 2015, a new public space called Keel Square was opened in Sunderland with the main feature being a unique art structure entitled 'The Keel Line'. This structure runs the length of the Naess Crusader and includes a strip of paving with the names of over 8,100 ships launched on the River Wear carved into the granite.

"Ships are the nearest things to...

DREAMS

...that hands have ever made,

for somewhere deep in their oaken hearts the...

SOUL

...of a song is laid"

- Robert N. Rose

"My Dad, George William Renton, worked in the Shipyards and my eldest brother George worked on the Tugs back in the day. I saw my first ship launch at the age of seven, the huge Bulk Carrier Orenda Bridge from JL Thompson's yard, 3rd November 1971.

She was the largest ship built in Sunderland at the time and a truly magnificent sight to witness, which stays with me to this day, still so vividly in my mind. This sparked my almost lifelong interest in Sunderland's Tugs and Shipbuilding history over the years. Both my Dad and George always told me about upcoming launches in the coming few years.

I developed an even more healthy interest when I learned that there was going to be an even bigger ship built at JL's yard. The next launch I got to see was Naess Crusader on 21st December 1972, a massive 158,000 tonne OBO (Oil/Bulk/Ore) Carrier .

I remember running down to the riverside after school almost every day that year to watch her progress on the slipway at JL's yard on the other side of the Wear at the East End Quayside. I drew regular pictures of her under construction at JL's at home as she looked at the time, wish I still had these now!

The launch day, 21st December was very cold and dull, almost dark when she slid down the ways at about 3.30 pm. I remember complaining when I was led home as I wanted to stay and see her towed to the Manor Quay. Dad said that we weren't going to stay here for another 2 hours!

The whole experience of seeing her from Keel laying to launch, seeing her grow during fitting out and watching her leave the Wear for trials and then return with problems with welding cracking really sticks with me.

She anchored off the Wear (as she was deemed too big to bring back into the Wear safely) as Tugs took welding crews out to fix her. Me and a couple of friends stood on a wall behind the Welcome Tavern and sang a little song to her while saluting...8 year olds eh?!"

Anthony Renton
Founder of 'Sunderland tugs and shipbuilding in pictures'
www.facebook.com/SunderlandTugs

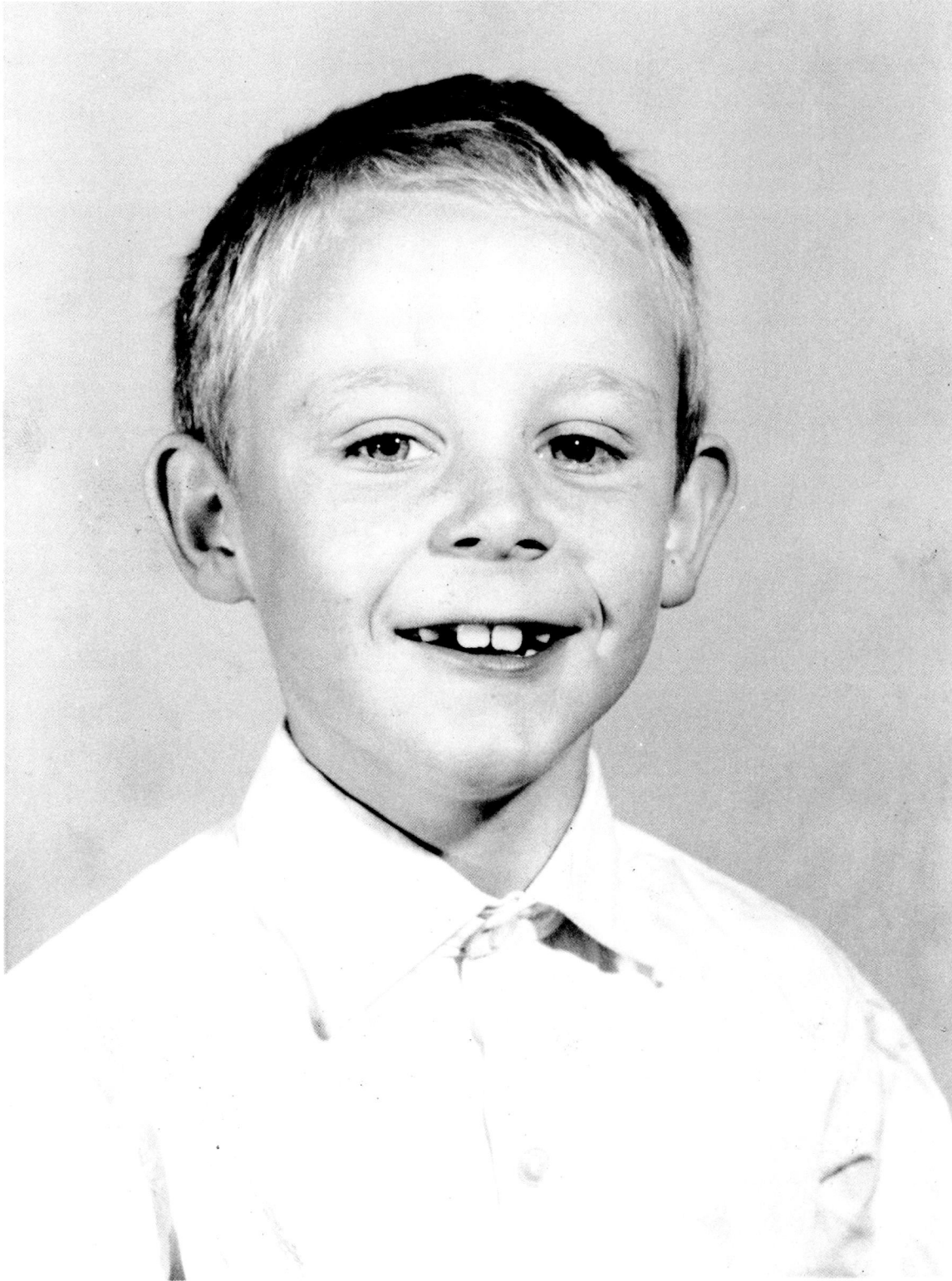

Anthony Renton at the age of 8

December 21st 1972:
The Naess Crusader under tow to the fitting out yard at Manor
Quay by the tugs Marsden, Prestwick and Westsider.
The tugs to the right of the picture are the Whitburn and Cornhill.

(TWAM ref. DT.TUR/2/60988A)

63

4 March 1973
Aerial view of 'Naess Crusader' at Manor Quay,
Sunderland as a ship is towed past. The image
also shows her sister ship 'Nordic Chieftain'
under construction at the North Sands shipyard.
The vessel under tow has been identified as
'Fidias' (launched at the Deptford yard,
Sunderland on 18 December 1972) by Anthony
Renton of Sunderland Tugs and Shipbuilding in
pictures.

(TWAM ref. DT.TUR/2/61267B)

June 1973
Aerial starboard stern quarter view of the OBO
carrier 'Naess Crusader' on sea trials.

(TWAM ref. DT.TUR/6/61816G).

"I was born in 1964 and brought up in Hendon, Sunderland. Most of my family worked in the shipbuilding and ship repair industries. If they didn't then it was on the tugboats or in merchant shipping. My dad was a plumber in the yards and probably worked in every one of them. He served his time at T.W. Greenwells' ship repair yard on the South Dock. His father and grandfather had also worked down there.

As a kid my dad would bring all sorts home for me to play with: offcuts of copper and steel pipe, ball bearings, Conex and Yorkshire pipe fittings, turned metalwork from lathes, nuts and bolts and the odd spanner or other hand tools. I was also given what was left of his bait: half a corned beef sandwich and a Bar Six or Kit Kat. I would be quite happy to play for hours with the nuts and bolts and small lengths of pipe on the floor in the living room.

When I left school at sixteen, with zero qualifications, I decided to enroll on a course at Wearside College of Further Education. The course was run by the Manpower Services Commission and entitled "Introduction to Engineering". The course lasted six months and I loved it. Everything was crammed in over this short time; from the use of basic hand tools such as hacksaws, files, micrometers and Vernier gauges, to welding and the use of metal work lathes. Everything you needed to know to get a start was included.

When the six months was up, off I went looking for work, full of confidence and thinking I could do anything... young and daft as they say. A couple of weeks later it would be knocked out of me and I would learn the hard way! Among the few letters I mailed, one was addressed to Mr. Thomas Benson of the Wear Dock Engineering Company Limited, South Dock, Sunderland. To my surprise I was offered an interview.

When the day came I took the bus down wearing my new suit. I stepped off the bus at Barrack Street and asked the security fella where to go. "Down the dock bank, over the swing bridge, turn right and the buildings on your left." Passing a few ships of various sizes, tug boats and a few blokes taking the mickey out of my suit I found the place. Mrs. Benson called me into the office. I sat down in front of Mr. Benson, a rough looking fella who didn't mess about…

"Why do you want to work here?"
-        "My dad works in the yards and I'd like to do the same."
"What does your dad do in the yards?"
-        "He's a plumber and I'd like to do the same."
"We don't need any plumbers. I'll put you in with the platers and see how you get on. Okay?"
-        "Yeah. Fine"
"Okay. You start Monday. Get yersel' to the Army & Navy Stores and buy two boilersuits. Then go to Strothers. You'll need to buy a six inch and two-foot rule and square. What size boot do you take?"
-        "Ten"
"Okay. I'll buy them for you. You can pay me back weekly. Okay?"
-        "Yeah"
"Right. See you Monday. Be here for quarter past eight. See you then."

That was it. I had just signed up for an apprenticeship.

Monday came around and by strange coincidence I was told to work with Alan Bell, a plumber who had worked in the yards with my Dad. First job: helping to put up an overhead travelling crane about 40 feet up. I was given all sorts of odd jobs and menial tasks at first and was slowly drafted in to work with the platers. A great bunch of fellas once you got to know them but they didn't mess around and didn't take crap from anyone. The main job at the time was construction of a coal drilling rig for the ship 'Wimpey Geocore'. The whole thing was completed without most of the necessary equipment, it was all down to hard graft and common sense.

In the summer it was too hot and winters were too cold. As it was only about thirty yards from the sea wall, the spray used to come in through the broken windows during winter. In winter 1982 the dock froze over! I went through a load of boilersuits as you couldn't wash them: they were saturated with grime from working in boilers or the double bottoms.

The work was interesting as we built all sorts for marine applications and other areas of industry. People used to work as a team and we always got the job done right first time. Texaco were even kind enough to send me a letter of thanks for making a replacement anchor winch. As the years went by the place never changed. After the rig was finished a lot of the blokes got work elsewhere. I guess some of them had had enough of the working conditions. Health and Safety was non-existent, you just got on with it. We had to do jobs that were outlawed a few years later: welding galvanised pipe and working around asbestos. I was paid £36:40 for a 40-hour week after national insurance.

I have to say that when I left I missed the blokes but not the working conditions. At this time, everyone had a feeling that the yards were going to close. Everyone noticed the drop in orders and yards closing one-by-one. Through the lack of engineering jobs in the area I ventured further afield working in places like Kent and Wiltshire. Anyway, the yards closed thanks to one particular woman and her cohorts. The town had lost its main industries and now we have only one yard left.

When built, Doxford's was the largest covered shipyard in the world and funnily enough, I'm working there now. In Bay 3 we are restoring the Senora, a 108 year-old motor yacht designed by Alfred Mylne and built on the Isle of Bute. It's all voluntary, we're getting the kids in to teach them new skills and they seem to be enjoying it. In a way it's nice to be back in familiar surroundings with the machinery and the odd ghost looking over your shoulder. Unfortunately no ships are being built there now. The local politicians and those in Parliament don't have an interest and at low tide you can walk across the river due to lack of dredging. With a bit of investment it could be a working yard again. But then again, what do we know, eh?"

Don Simpson
Former Shipyard worker

March 2018
View of the Queen Alexandra
Bridge from the rear of Doxford's
sheds. The Stadium of Light can
just be seen in the background.

The true poem is the...

POET'S

...mind, the true...

SHIP

...is the...

SHIP
BUILDER

- Ralph Waldo Emerson

March 2018
One of the control decks of the machinery at Doxford's as it looks today.

1   2   3   4

$ % & ' ( ) Ø * = PAGE
4 5 6 7 8 9 0

TAPE ←TAPE   TAB   LINE   RETURN
R T Y U I Ō P   FEED

EOT   @   RUB
D F G H J K L FORM + OUT RESET BREAK

                              ?
C V B ^N M < > / SHIFT

PAINT ROOM

NO SMOKING

CAUTION
MEN
WORKING
BELOW

A community is like a...

SHIP

...everyone ought to be prepared to take the...

HELM

- Henrik Ibsen

F.R.

195

kgs

'The future of Shipbuilding in the North East'

Today there are signs all over the City of the once bustling shipbuilding industry but the original yards have more or less disappeared, been demolished and new buildings have replaced them.

However, one yard remains in the shadow of the Queen Alexandra Bridge. Doxford's yard doesn't look much different from the day it closed in 1989 but it feels more like a ghost town. Now home to thousands of pigeons and seagulls it is rented by a number of different businesses.

The dry dock now stands empty as the UK, having once been the industry leader in shipbuilding, finds that this is now a millstone around its neck, because of the political issues that accompanied the decline and people are still understandably bitter about this.

In early 2017 the UK National Shipbuilding Strategy was published for the Government by Sir John Parker who was once the Managing Director of Austin & Pickersgill in Sunderland in 1974.

It is hoped his recommendations to transform the UK's shipbuilding industry and boost the prosperity of shipyards across the country will be taken up by the government but so far we are yet to see any evidence of this on Wearside although, on the Tyne, the A&P yard has recently been responsible for building the huge stern section for the RRS Sir David Attenborough, a flagship polar research vessel which was affectionately named 'Boaty McBoatface' by many!

To be honest it's unlikely the industry will suddenly rise again like a phoenix from the flames as the attention of the current Government is focused on looking at post Brexit development.

However, this book is not about blame or what could have been done to save the shipbuilding industry; instead we need to celebrate what the City has achieved and how it's moving forward in so many other aspects.

Although Sunderland didn't win their bid for Capital of Culture in 2021 the City has seen a renewed energy and enthusiasm for what the City does still have to offer.

I do believe the Tall Ships coming to the Wear in July is only the beginning of the most exciting few years for the City. As I mentioned in my introduction I always felt that Sunderland sat in the shadow of Newcastle for a long time and there was a feeling of lethargy because of that. However, I think the people of Sunderland should be proud of their history and use this pride to generate more interest and development in the City.

It has been my honour and privilege to really get to know the people of Sunderland over the past four years and I look forward to being a part of their exciting future.

FIRE EXIT
KEEP CLEAR

North East Shipbuilders Ltd

NE SL

EVACUATION OF SHIPS/SHEDS

WHEN ALARM SOUNDS

The Fire Alarms are:

1. Continuous Sounding of Time Buzzer

2. Portable Fire Alarms on Ship(s) (Break Glass type)

3. Supervisors to supplement this with the blowing of whistle

4. Fire Bells ringing in Sheds/Offices

ON HEARING ALARM

1. Leave Ship/Sheds immediately

2. Collect Disc Board from Rack

3. Proceed to Fire Point for Roll Call

your work area until instructed by

If my...

SHIP

...sails from sight, it doesn't mean my...

JOURNEY

...ends, it simply means the...

RIVER BENDS

- John Enoch Powell

"My Dad, George William Renton was born in Burleigh Street in the East End of Sunderland in 1923. He volunteered to join the Royal Navy in 1940 during the war, serving on quite a few ships including the battleship HMS Nelson, aircraft carrier HMS Illustrious and battleship HMS Vanguard, returning home in 1950.

He worked in various yards on the Wear as a Rigger; he was an excellent Seaman who knew almost everything about splicing ropes and wires, which was perfect for his job. He was hugely proud of his hometown and its shipbuilding history and that rubbed off on me from a very young age.

I always remember talking to him about the future in 1978. I was due to be given careers advice at school that year and I said that I wanted to join the Wear Tugs like my big brother George or get a job in the yards. His answer shocked me, he said to me "I wouldn't bother Son, it will all be gone in another 10 years, find yourself something with a long term future. If you like the history of it all, maybe a Maritime Historian?"

My Dad passed away aged 65 in 1988, the year the last shipyard closed its doors forever. I so wish he was still here now to see the page I've set up, he would have absolutely loved it!"

Anthony Renton
Founder of 'Sunderland tugs and shipbuilding in pictures'
www.facebook.com/SunderlandTugs

George Renton stood next to the Montana at Greenwell's yard in 1962. The Montana was built at Laing's yard. Launched 5th September 1960 and completed in 1961. She was the largest ever ship to fit in Greenwell's No2 drydock, hence George's arm on her bow emphasising the tight fit. The Montana was broken up on 28th February 1987, a year before the last shipyard closed in Sunderland.

Vessel Type: Oil tanker
Length: 559ft 3in

The heavy industries that shaped the..

NORTH

...also shaped the emotional lives

Winding towers and cranes can be torn

...formed through shared hardship

LIVE

OF ENGLAND

of the generations of...

PEOPLE

...who lived there.

down in a day, but the...

BONDS

working under them...

ON

- Grayson Perry
The Vanity in Small Differences

2: TALL SHIPS

Killoran as she was towed towards the harbour under full sail on June 13, 1932. Built by Ailsa Shipbuilding Company of Troon in 1900, the 1,757 gross-ton three-masted Killoran was one of the last trade sailing tall ships to visit Sunderland.

KILLORAN

A sailing vessel is...

ALIVE

in a way that no ship with mechanical...

POWER *...ever be*

- Aubrey de Selincourt

Torrens
Nationality: United Kingdom
Year built: 1875
Type of vessel: clipper ship
Length: 222ft 1 inches
Designed to carry 1st and 2nd class passengers & cargo
between the UK and Australia.

'The Mighty Torrens'

In 1875 the clipper ship, Torrens, was built in Sunderland by James Laing. She was a square rigged, three masted ship designed to carry passengers and cargo between London and Adelaide in South Australia and became known as the fastest ship to sail on that route.

The reason for this was that she was the only vessel for years with telescopic studding sail booms (a studding sail is an extra sail hoisted alongside a square-rigged sail on an extension of its yard arm.) which enabled her to capture even the lightest breeze, and therefore reach her destination so much faster than other ships of her time.

The Captain of the Torrens was Henry Robert Angel who had specified how she should be built and was a major shareholder in the costs for building her. He had devised a secret way to furl and unfurl the studding sails easily and quickly when others had failed.

The Australian clippers were bound for the most dangerous, stormy waters on the planet - the Southern Oceans featuring mountainous seas; however, this was the route chosen by these intrepid sailors as the winds in these oceans created record runs of 300 to 350 miles a day, by sheer wind power alone.

The Torrens survived these perilous oceans for the first fifteen years until Captain Angel retired and she was passed to the command of Captain Falkland Angel, Henry's son.

Under the captainship of Falkland Angel, the Torrens was never sailed with the same degree of success that his father had, and it was whilst under his command that she struck a massive iceberg in dense fog in 1899.

She was dismasted, had her bow stoved in and lost her bowsprit and figurehead. After being repaired and restored she was sold to Italian owners in 1903 before eventually being scrapped in 1910.

That could have been the end of the story; however, in 1973 two Australian Antarctic research expeditioners found the headless, but otherwise perfect, full sized female figurehead during a survey of Macquarie Island (South West of New Zealand). The figurehead was believed to be based on Flores Angel the daughter of Henry Angel.

Researchers believe this was the figurehead lost from the Torrens in 1899 so she was eventually transported to the Queen Victoria Museum in Launceston, Tasmania where she is preserved.

The headless figurehead
Photo credit: Bob Thompson

Tasmanian Parks and Wildlife Officer,
Irenej Skira with the figurehead at Skua
Lake, 1974.

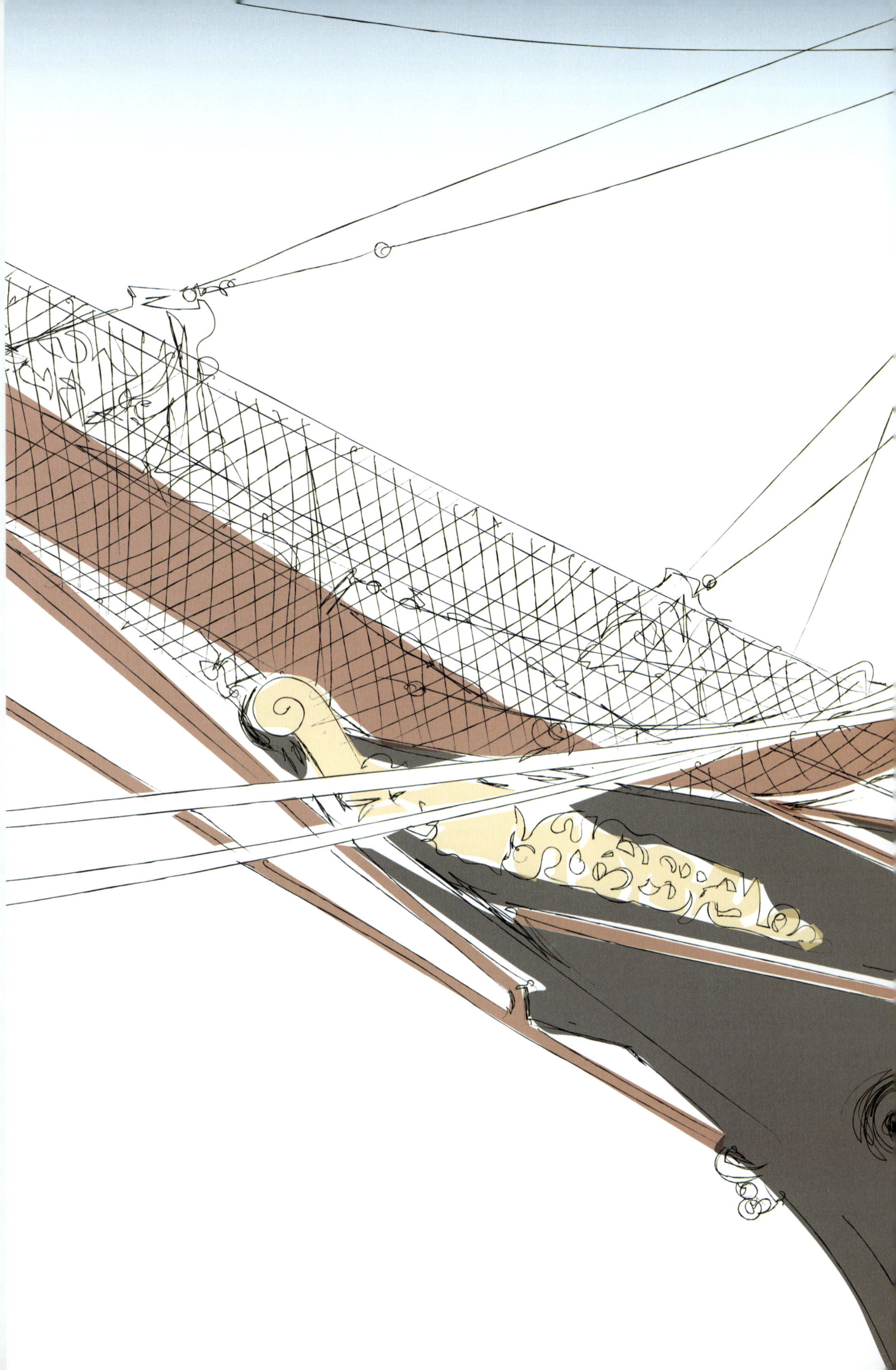

STS SEDOV

Launched in Kiel in 1921 at the Krupp yard, **Sedov** (then named Magdalene Vinnen), the four masted sail training barque of the University of Murmansk is used to train young cadets at the University to become officers, mechanics and radio specialists.

In 1936, Magdalene Vinnen was sold to Norddeutscher Lloyd, Bremen and was renamed Kommodore Johnsen. She undertook a number of circumnavigations, transporting wheat, coal and cereal.

The Second World War put an end to transporting this cargo, however she continued to train cadets in the Baltic where her journeys lasted from five to six weeks.

After the surrender of Germany she came under Russian state ownership and was renamed "Sedov" after the polar explorer Georgij Sedov who died during an investigation in the Arctic in 1914.

Sedov was used as an oceanographical vessel until 1966 then throughout the 70's she had a number of refits. She finally left the shipyard in 1981 and starting taking cadets from the naval schools of Kalingrad and Murmansk.

The fall of the Wall in 1989 and the Proclamation of Independence of Latvia in 1991 influenced the fate of Sedov. She headed for Murmansk, her new port of registry and was bought by Murmansk naval school who are responsible for her maintenance and upkeep.

She participates regularly in the majority of the big maritime international events and has been a regular participant in the Tall Ships' Races since the late 80's.
For more information visit: *www.sts-sedov.info/eng/*

Nationality: Russia
Year built: 1920
Type of vessel: 4 masted Barque 4
LOA exc. bowsprit: 356ft 7 inches
Number of trainees: 140
Number of permanent crew: 70

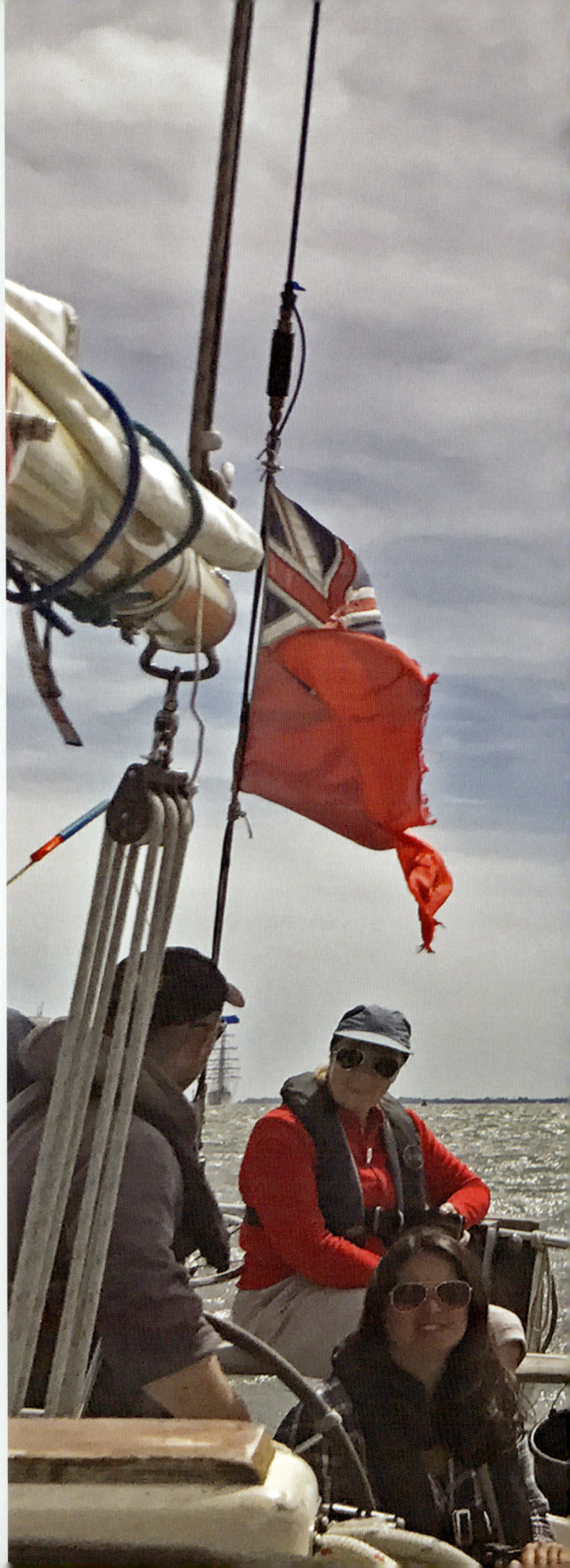

August 2017
View from the Black Diamond of Durham
looking back towards the Sedov passing us on
the 'port' or left side in the Szczecin Lagoon

It's not the...

SHIP

...so much as the skilful...

SAILING

...that assures the prosperous voyage.

- George William Curtis

СЕДОВ

КАЛИНИНГРАД

IMO 7946356

...*having little or no money in my purse, & nothing particular to interest me on...*

SHORE

...*I thought I would...*

SAIL

...*about a little and see the...*

WATERY

...*part of the...*

WORLD

- H Melville
Opening line from 'Moby Dick'

The Russian four-masted barque **Kruzenshtern** (Russian: Барк Крузенштерн) is the World's second largest traditional sailing ship after the Sedov. She was built in 1926 in Bremerhaven-Wesermünde, Germany as one of five clipper ships for the "Flying P Line" which traded in the Atlantic, Indian Ocean and Pacific.

The five ships' names all began with "P", with the Kruzenshtern originally named Padua, and she is the only one of the five still sailing today. Pamir was caught in Hurricane Carrie in 1957 and sank off the Azores, with only six survivors rescued after an extensive search; Peking ended up as a museum in New York before returning to Germany in 2017 where she is undergoing a three year refurbishment which may see her sail again; Pommern is now a museum ship belonging to the Åland Maritime Museum and is anchored in western Mariehamn and Passat is now a youth hostel, venue, museum ship, and landmark moored at Travemünde near the Kiel Canal.

Padua was given to Russia in 1946 and renamed Kruzenshtern after the famous early 19th century Baltic German explorer in Russian service, Adam Johann Krusenstern.

She is easy to recognise painted in a distinctive black with a wide white stripe with black rectangles, common on ships that traded with the East, where the design imitated gunports to scare away pirates.
For more information visit:
www.kruzenshtern.info

Nationality: Russia
Year built: 1926
Type of vessel: 4 masted Square rigged barque
LOA: 341ft 6 inches
Number of trainees: 179
Number of permanent crew: 61

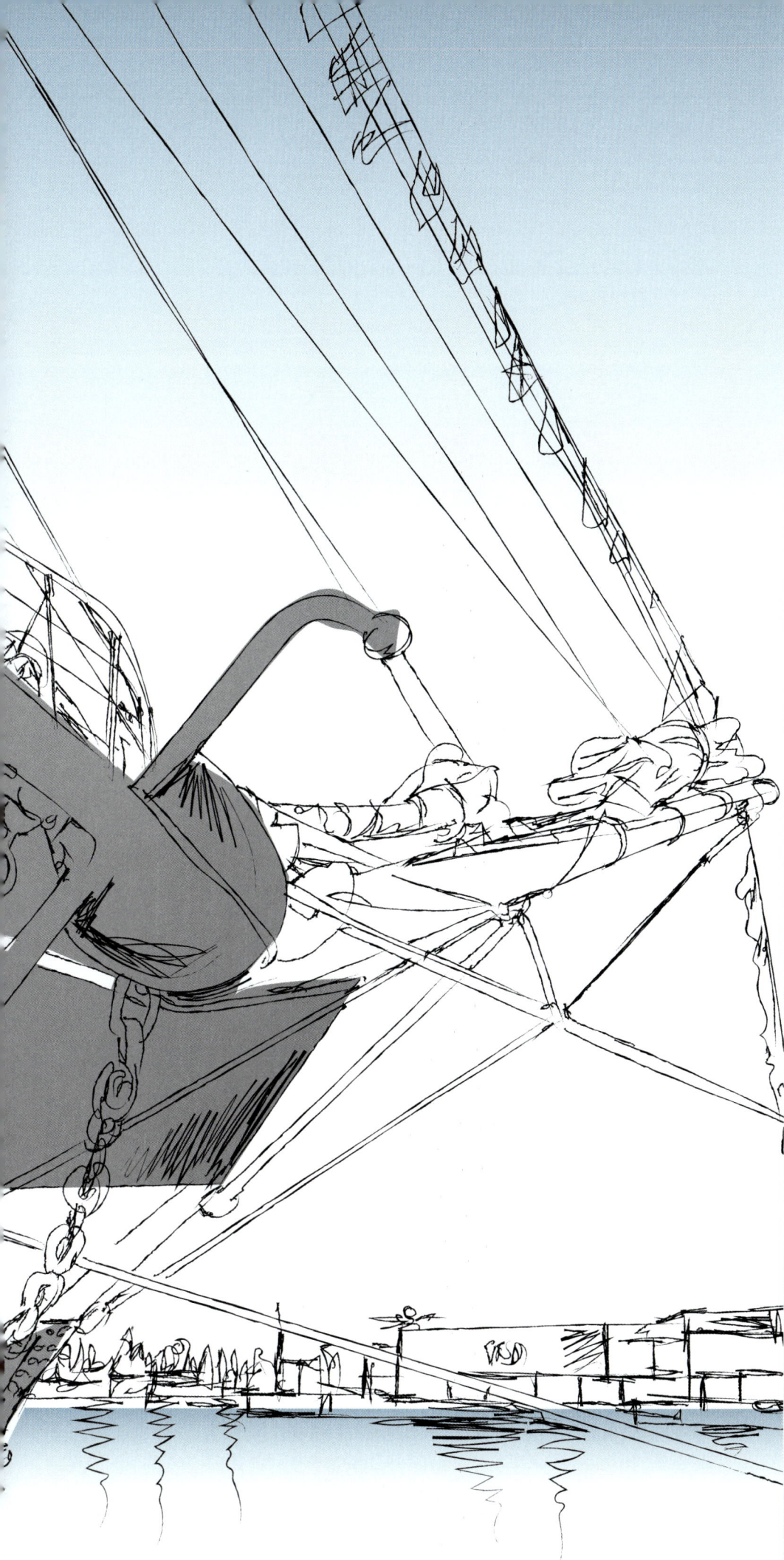

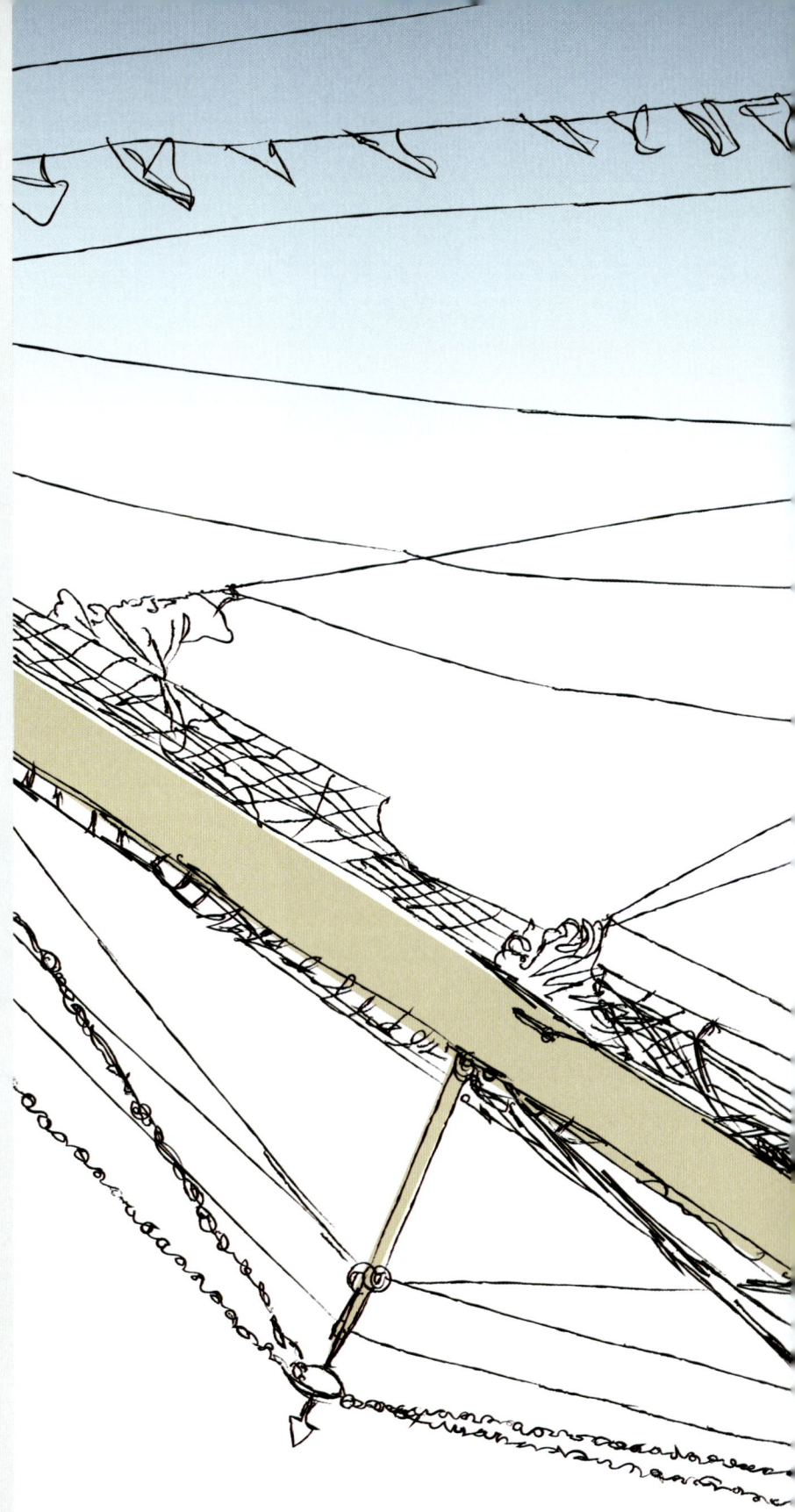

The bow of the Mir
The bow is the forward part of the hull of a ship or boat. The bow is designed to reduce the resistance of the hull cutting through water and should be high enough to prevent water from easily washing over the top of it.

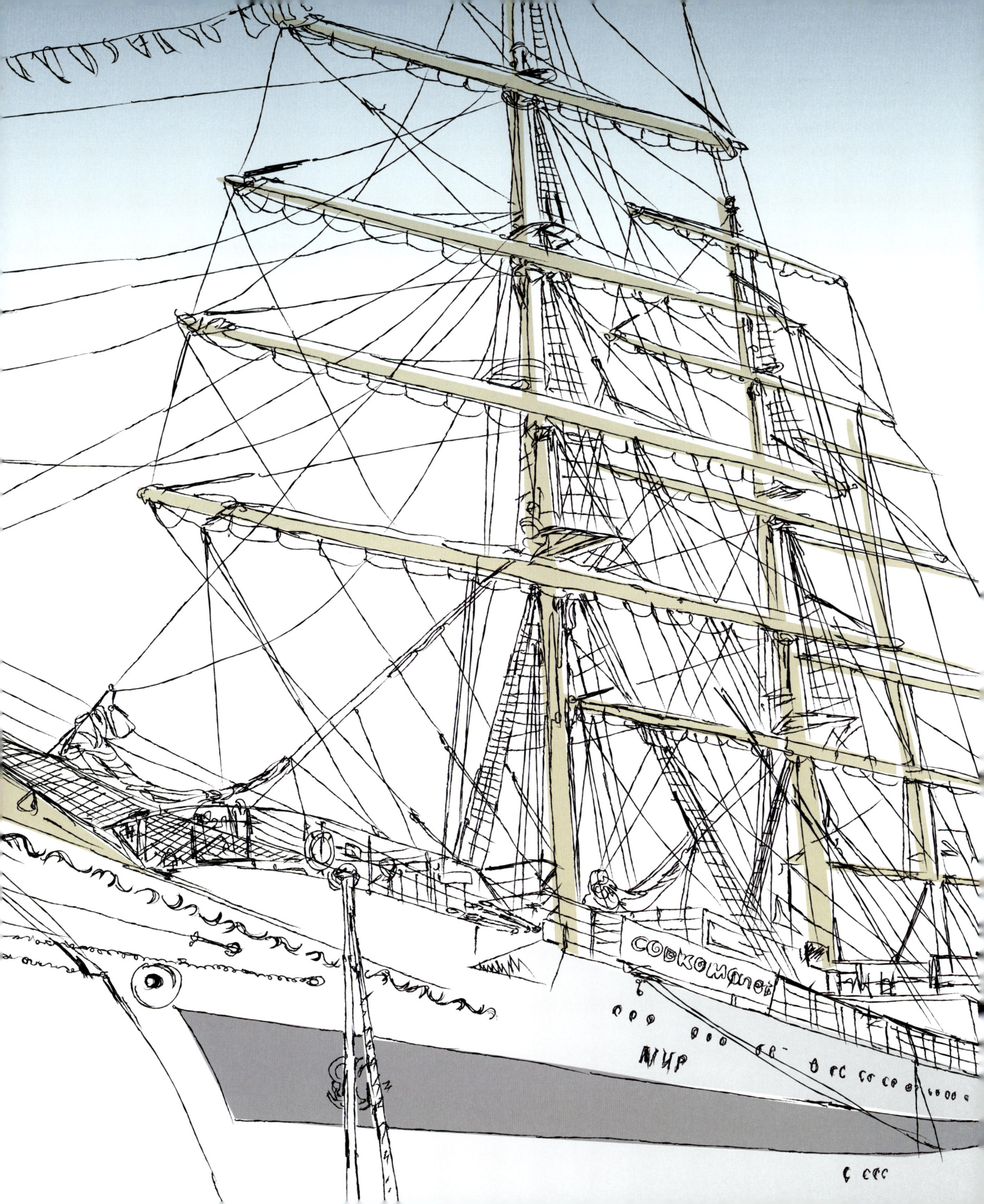

STS Mir (Russian: Mup, meaning Peace)

Mir is a three-masted, full rigged training ship, based in St. Petersburg, Russia. She is owned by Admiral Makarov State Maritime Academy (AMSMA) in Saint Petersburg who operate Mir as its main training vessel.

She was built in 1987 at the Lenin Shipyard in Gdańsk, Poland as the third of six sister ships designed by Polish naval architect Zygmunt Choreń; she is the second largest of the six weighing 2,385 tonnes. Her sister ships are the Dar Młodzieży, Druzhba, Pallada, Khersones, and Nadezhda.

Her main mast is 170 feet high and, along with the other masts supports a total sail area of 2,771 m2. Mir is 26 feet shorter than the second longest current sailing ship, the STS Sedov.

The ship was built as a cadet training ship, designed to carry between 70 and 144 cadets. In addition to her training role, the Academy now also offer sailing trips, daytrips and "cruises" on a commercial basis; giving the experience of sailing on Mir to those outside of Russia.

Mir has taken part in many races, including the annual Tall Ships' Races, winning various prizes. Mir came out as the absolute winner in the Grand Regatta Columbus 1992 which celebrated the discovery of America by Christopher Columbus in 1492.

Nationality: Russia
Year built: 1987
Type of vessel: M108 class full rigged 3 masted ship
LOA exc. bowsprit: 311ft
Number of trainees: 144
Number of permanent crew: 55

STS MIR

The bowsprit of the Mir showing the gold intricate detail below.

The bowsprit of a ship is a spar extending forward from the vessel's prow. It provides an anchor point for the forestay(s), allowing the fore-mast to be stepped farther forward on the hull. The word bowsprit is thought to originate from the Middle Low German word *bōchsprēt* - *bōch* meaning bow and *sprēt* meaning pole

The gangway up to the Mir.
A gangway is a narrow passage used to
board or disembark ships. These generally
move up and down depending on the tide
so it can either quite flat or rather steep.

You can never cross the... **OCEAN** *unless you have the courage to lose sight of the...* **SHORE**

— Christopher Columbus

Shtandart (Russian: Штандартъ) is an exact replica of the first ship of Russia's Baltic fleet which was launched in 1703 at the Olonetsky shipyard near Olonets by the decree of Tsar Peter I and orders issued by commander Aleksandr Menshikov. The name Shtandart was also given to the royal yachts of the tsars until the Russian Revolution in 1917. Tsar Nicholas II's royal yacht was the last of this series.

The replica Shtandart was launched at the Petrovsky Shipyard in St Petersburg in 1999 as a functional training ship. In June 2000 the Shtandart set sail on her maiden voyage. The frigate retraced the route taken by Peter I, during his Grand Embassy; a Russian diplomatic mission to Western Europe in 1697–98 with the primary goal to strengthen and broaden the Holy League, Russia's alliance with a number of European countries against the Ottoman Empire in its struggle for the north coastline of the Black Sea.

From her launch to the end of 2017 the Shtandart has sailed approximately 150,000 nautical miles in the Baltic, North, Norwegian Barents and Mediterranean Seas, as well as sailing to Canary Islands. She has visited one hundred and fifty ports in seventeen countries. Nearly 7000 trainees from 27 countries have experienced an adventure on board Shtandart. The ship's motto is *Life is what you make it.*
For more information visit:
www.shtandart.ru/en/frigate

Nationality: Russia
Year built: 1999
Type of vessel: square rigged 3 masted frigate
Length: 83ft 8in
Number of trainees: 32
Number of permanent crew: 8

STS SHTANDART

The stern is the back of a ship or boat.
The stern end of a ship is indicated
with a white navigation light at night.

Штандартъ

Санктъ-Петербургъ

DAR MLODZIEZY

Dar Młodzieży (Polish: Gift of Youth) is a Polish sail training ship designed by Zygmunt Choreń. A prototype of a class of six, the following five slightly-differing units were built subsequently by the same shipyard for the merchant fleet of the former Soviet Union. Her sister ships are Mir, Druzhba, Pallada, Khersones and Nadezhda.

The ship was launched in November 1981 at the Gdańsk shipyard, Poland, and commissioned for service in July 1982 at Gdynia, thus replacing her forerunner Dar Pomorza. Her home port is Gdynia.

The Dar Młodzieży is the first Polish-built, ocean-going sailing vessel to circumnavigate the globe (1987–88), thus repeating the famous voyage of her predecessor (1934–35).

Nationality: Poland
Year built: 1982
Type of vessel: full rigged 3 masted ship
LOA exc. bowsprit: 311ft
Number of trainees: 136
Number of permanent crew: 32

STS DAR MŁODZIEŻY

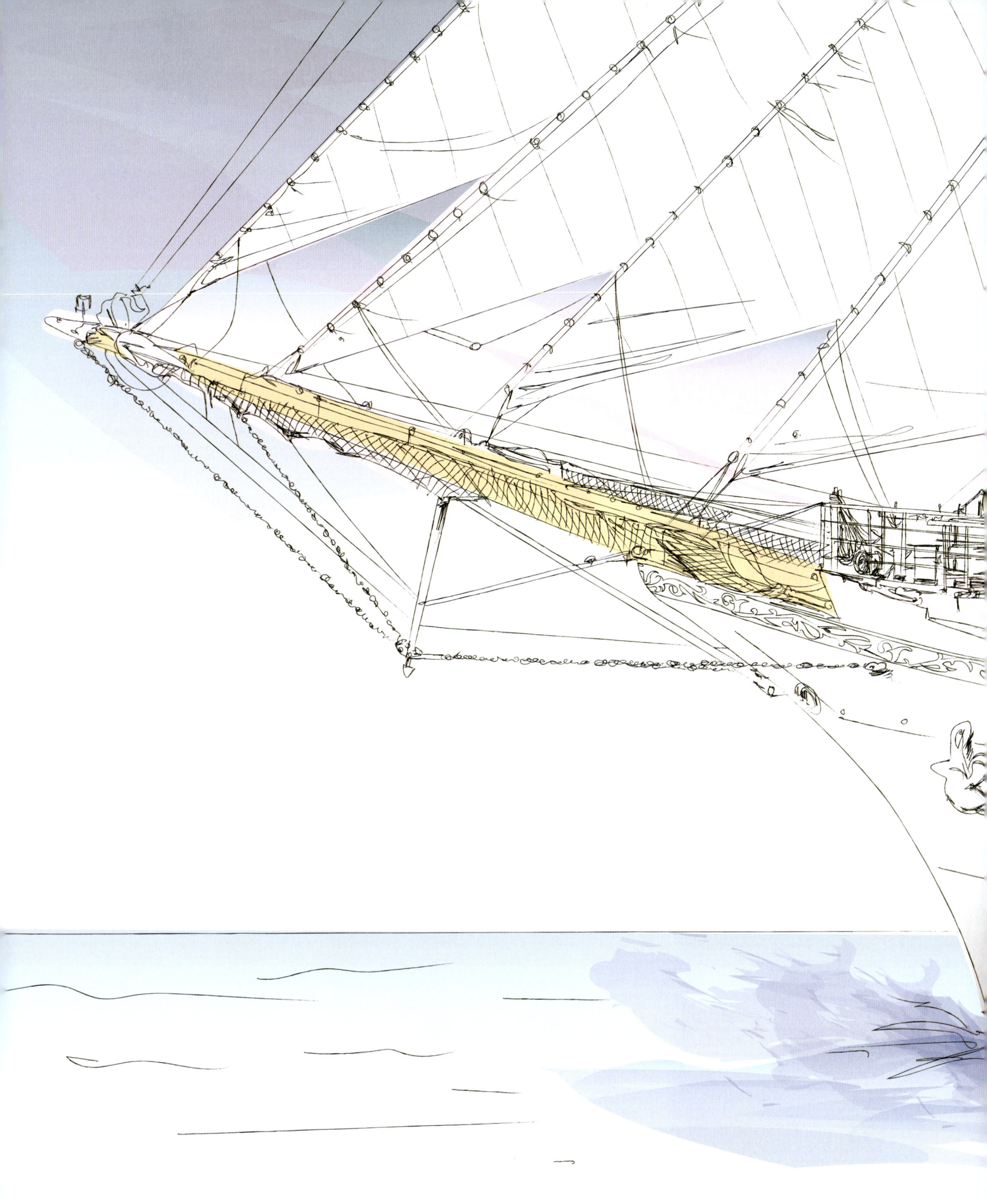

DAR MŁODZIEŻY

Tenacious is one of only two vessels of their type in the world (the other being Lord Nelson) designed and built to be fully accessible for people over 16 years old with disabilities or impairments (including wheelchair users).

Her owners, the Jubilee Sailing Trust have strived to enable people of all physical abilities to sail. In the early 1990's it was becoming clear that this mission was becoming increasingly popular. Their other ship, Lord Nelson, commissioned and specifically designed for the Trust, was unable to continue to supply the growing demand. With initial funding secured in 1995 (including 65% from the National Lottery) the project to build a new ship for the JST got fully underway.

On 3rd of February 2000 Tenacious left the Jubilee Yard (Merlin Quay) in Southampton where she was built and on the 6th of April 2000 she was officially named in a ceremony attended by HRH The Duke of York. She was the largest wooden ship to be built in the UK for over 100 years.

Tenacious undertook her maiden voyage 1,548 days after her keel was laid, on 1st September 2000 from Southampton to Southampton calling at Sark, St Helier and Weymouth. For more information visit: *www.jst.org.uk*

Nationality: UK
Year built: 2000
Type of vessel: square rigged 3 masted barque
LOA exc. bowsprit: 177ft 2in
Number of trainees: 44
Number of permanent crew: 8

STS TENACIOUS

Leila is a rare example from the heyday of yacht racing. Built out of solid mahogany in Greenwich in 1892 by F. Wilkinson of Charlton, London for Mr. Leonard Withers of 53 Hamilton Road, Ealing, Middlesex, a member of the Temple Yacht Club; she is the oldest and smallest boat in the Tall Ships Race.

Her original owner kept her for 21 years and won the Round Britain yacht race in 1904. After a number of owners & adventures she was gifted to The Leila Sailing Trust in August 2008. The Trust was formed by Rob Bull and David Beavan to restore her for sail training.

The Trusts vision: *"We believe that all young people, regardless of circumstance or ability should have the opportunity to realise their true potential in order for them to live healthy, fulfilling lives – making a positive contribution to their community and to society in general."*

Although it's a small crew they become involved in everything, it's more like being part of a family. Leila celebrated reaching the grand old age of 125 in 2017.
For more information visit:
www.leila2c.org

Nationality: UK
Year built: 1892
Type of vessel: Gaff Cutter
LOA exc. bowsprit: 42ft 7 inches
Number of trainees: 6
Number of permanent crew: 3

STS LEILA

Throw off the bowlines,
sail away from the safe harbour...

EXPLORE

DREAM

DISCOVER

- Mark Twain

Detail of the Rigging on the Skonnerten Jylland

Rigging comprises the system of ropes, cables and chains, which support a sailing ship or sail boat's masts.

The basis of all rigging is the mast, which may be composed of one or many pieces of wood or metal. The mast is supported by stays and shrouds that are known as the standing rigging because they are made fast.

The ropes by which the yards, on square riggers, the booms of fore-and-aft sails, and sails, such as jibs, are manipulated for trimming to the wind and for making or shortening sail are known as the running rigging.

ANDERSEN
28ST
TWO SPEED

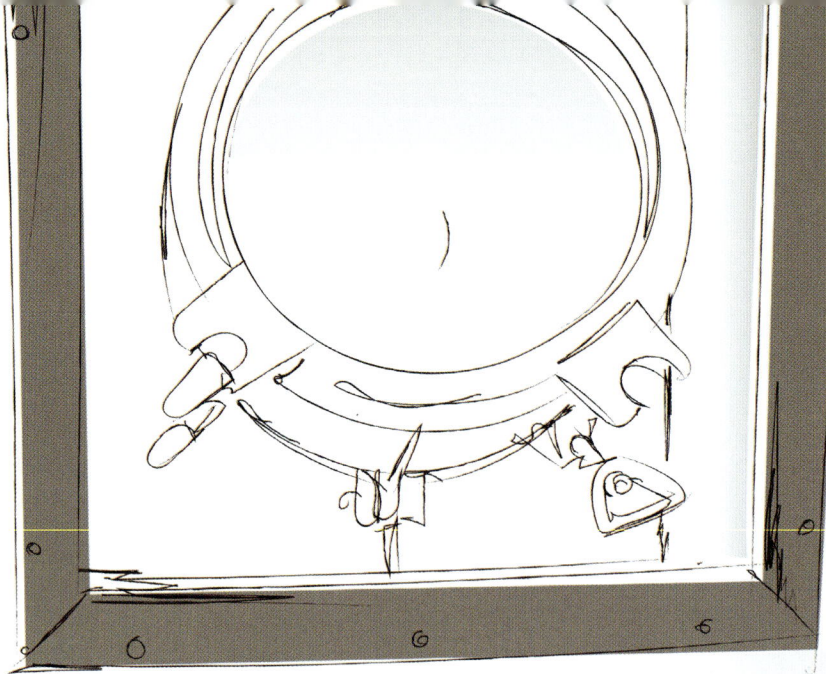

The toilets on a ship or boat are known as the **'heads'**. This term evolves from the days of sailing ships when the place for the crew to relieve themselves was all the way at the front of the ship on either side of the bowsprit. A sailing vessel cannot travel directly into the wind. The one location that is always downwind is the head or bow end. The wind would always blow along the deck towards the stern which would carry most of the odour away. If you've ever been downwind of a field full of cows it makes sense why the toilet was positioned upwind!

In sailing ships, the toilet was placed in the bow above the water line with vents or slots cut near the floor level allowing normal wave action to wash out the facility. Only the captain had a private toilet near his quarters, at the stern of the ship.

In many modern boats with the various forms of engine power and manual or powered pumps, the 'head' can be anywhere, but the name stuck. On ships of today the 'heads' look similar to seated flush toilets but use a system of valves and pumps that brings sea water into the toilet and pumps the waste out through the hull in place of the more normal cistern and plumbing trap to a drain. In small boats the pump is often hand operated. The pump on a marine toilet operates in a "wet" mode and a "dry" mode. The cleaning mechanism can become easily blocked if too much toilet paper or other material is put down the pan.

The 'head' on the Skonnerten Jylland. The bucket is used to flush out the toilet when at sea.

A **figurehead** is a carved wooden decoration found at the bow of a ship, generally of a design related to the name or role of the ship. Since the beginning of civilisation the sea has always been something of a mystery to people. Seamen were superstitious so before the 16th century ships often had some form of bow ornamentation usually with the protective function to ward off evil spirits.

Between the 16th and 20th century figureheads were introduced and depicted a very important part of seamanship of the time. The beasts and Gods were substituted by mostly the figures of beautiful ladies and/or mythical creatures such as sirens or even saints and angels. For a long time it was still believed that a figurehead would lead the ship safely through troubled waters.

'Germany's Pride with 24 sails'
Alexander Von Humboldt II, or **'Alex 2'** as she is affectionately known by her crew, replaced her predecessor Alexander Von Humboldt in October 2011 to offer tall ship voyages and traditional seamanship for everyone, regardless of previous experience, but especially for young men and women aged 15-25. Based in her home port of Bremerhaven she is owned by the non profit organisation Deutsche Stiftung Sail Training (DSST).
For more information visit:
www.alex-2.de/

Nationality: Germany
Year built: 2011
Type of vessel: Square rigged 3 masted Barque
LOA exc. bowsprit: 187 feet
Number of trainees: 55
Number of permanent crew: 24

The **Eendracht (Dutch meaning: Unison)** is Holland's largest three-masted schooner. She was built in 1989 at the Damen shipyard based on a design by W. de Vries Lentsch. She is owned and operated by the Dutch Foundation Stichting Zeilschip and replaced her smaller predecessor Johann Schmidt.

Students from the Navigation and Transport College in Rotterdam are required to sail on the Eendracht for four days during the first year of their study.

The Eendracht has over 350 well trained, mostly voluntary, professional crew members. Every year she spends the winter months in the South, and the summer in the North Sea area.
For more information visit:
www.eendracht.nl/ship/the-ship

Nationality: Netherlands
Year built: 1989
Type of vessel: 3 masted Gaff schooner
LOA exc. bowsprit: 181ft 5in
Number of trainees: 39
Number of permanent crew: 15

STS EENDRACHT

The yards of the STS Sir Winston Churchill.
A yard is a spar on a mast from which sails are set.
The outermost tips of the yard are called the
yardarms. In order to set and stow the square sails,
the crew must climb aloft and spread out along the
yards. To do this, they stand in footropes suspended
beneath the yard and balance themselves between
that and the yard itself.

A smooth...

SEA

...never made a skilled...

SAILOR

- *John George Hermanson*

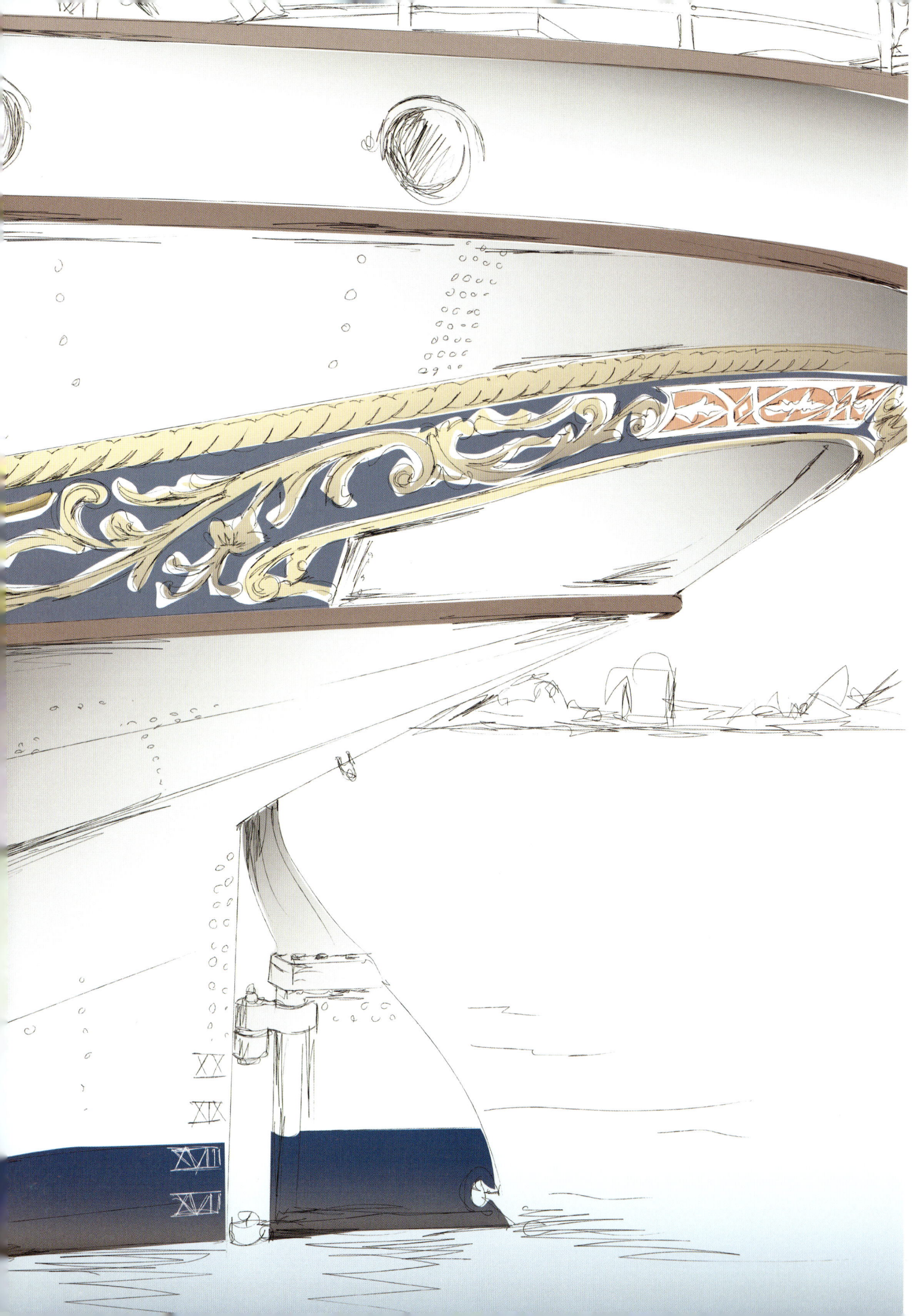

It's when you smell the breeze, taste the...

SALT

...and feel the...

WAVES

...beneath your feet that you

truly know that you are...

ALIVE

- Anthony T Hincks

Skonnerten Jylland.
Nationality: Denmark
Year built: 1951
Type of vessel: 3 masted topsail schooner
LOA exc. bowsprit: 102ft
Number of trainees: 18
Number of permanent crew: 7

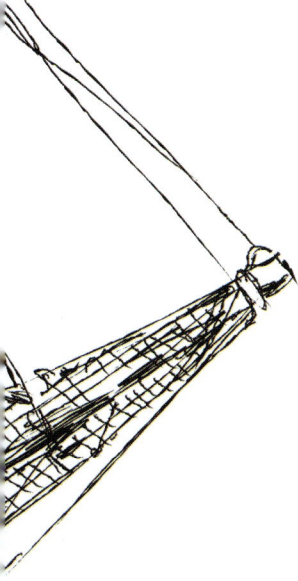

...all I ask is a...

TALL SHIP *and a...*

STAR

to steer her by.

- John Masefield

The Malcolm Miller as she looks today.
Fitted out as a luxury yacht she is still
entered into the Tall Ships Races

There is nothing, absolutely...

NOTHING

half so much worth doing as simply...

MESSING

...about in boats.

- Kenneth Grahame
The Wind in the Willows

STS BLACK DIAMOND OF DURHAM

Black Diamond of Durham was built in 1972. She was purchased by the Faramir Trust who stripped and refitted her for sail training in the North East of England in the early 1990's.

The Trust offered a sailing experience to young people from a disadvantaged background and since this date the boat has not missed a Tall Ships' Race.

In 1999 she was acquired by Sailing North East and was refitted again for a different type of client – Corporate Entertainment and Teambuilding alongside normal sail training.

The Black Diamond is based in Hartlepool and currently skippered by Calvyn Whitehand.

Nationality: United Kingdom
Year built: 1972
Type of vessel: Bowman Corsair Ocean Racer (BM Sloop)
LOA exc. bowsprit: 44ft 3 inches
Number of trainees: 8
Number of permanent crew: 2

159

March 2018
Black Diamond of Durham
Photo credit: Mike Shepherdson

Never in my life before have I experienced such...

BEAUTY

...and...

FEAR

...at the same time.

- Ellen MacArthur

I wanted...
FREEDOM,
...open air &...
ADVENTURE
I found it on the...
SEA

- Alain Gerbault

March 2018
Black Diamond of Durham
Photo credit: Mike Shepherdson

At...

SEA

...*I learned how little a person...*

NEEDS

...*not how much.*

- *Robin Lee Graham*

It is the set of the...

SAILS

...not the direction of the...

WIND

...that determines which way we will go.

– Jim Rohn

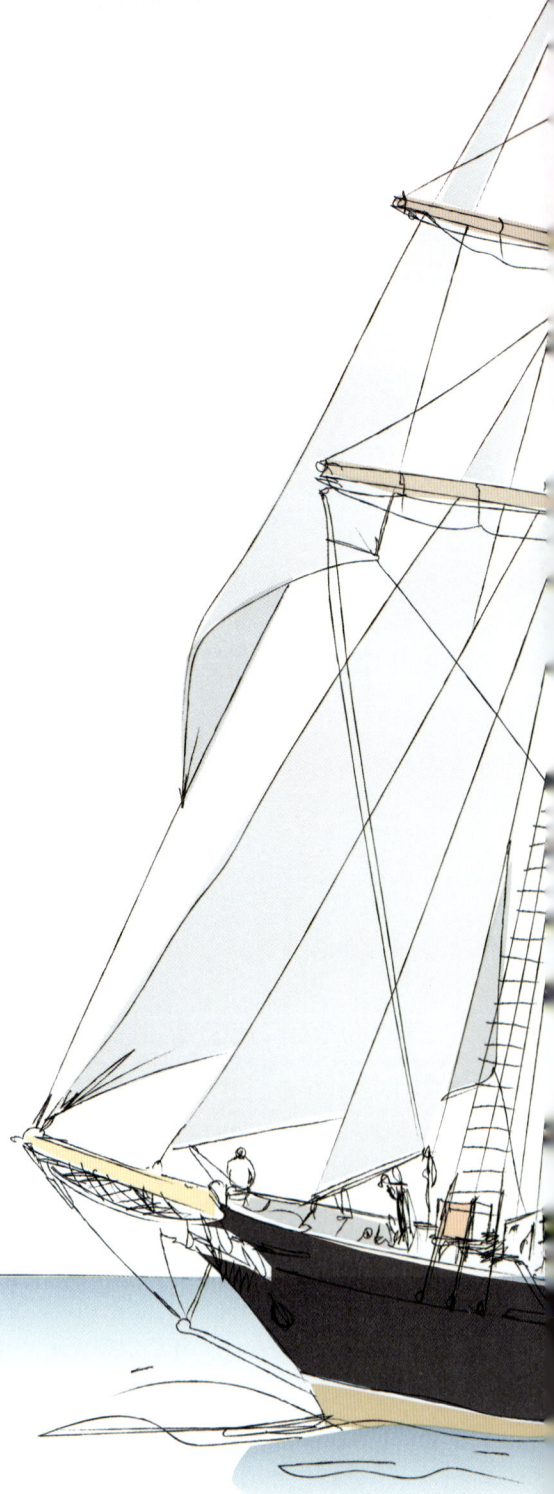

Sir Winston Churchill was commissioned by the Tall Ships Youth Trust, designed by Camper & Nicholson and built in 1966 to compete in the Tall Ships Race. Public donations partly funded construction of the ship and the Sail Training Association raised about half the needed money.

In 1968 her sister ship, Malcolm Miller was launched. Sir Winston Churchill differed from Malcolm Miller by having round topped cabin doors as opposed to square topped doors.

In 2000, Sir Winston Churchill was replaced in service by Prince William and sold by her owners, the Tall Ships Youth Trust. She is now serving as a private yacht off the Greek Islands.

Nationality: UK
Year built: 1966
Type of vessel: 3 masted topsail schooner
LOA: 150ft 3in
Number of trainees: 39
Number of permanent crew: 5

August 2017
The view from the stern of the Black Diamond of Durham in the middle of the Baltic Sea at 4.30am.
This photo was taken on my iphone and no filter was needed!

The crew of the Skonnerten Jylland back on board after the crew parade through the streets of Szczecin in Poland to celebrate the final of the Tall Ships Races 2018.

3: THE TALL SHIPS RACES
(and the life of a sail trainee)

The History of the Tall Ships Races

The Tall Ships Race was the brainchild of a retired London solicitor, Bernard Morgan, who wanted to foster understanding and friendly rivalry between young folk from around the World, and help to instil teamwork and determination, as well as giving them seafaring skills. As World War II came to an end, tall ships were a dying breed, having been replaced by more efficient steam-powered ships decades before therefore he thought this would be a fitting way to mark the end of the sailing era.

The Portuguese Ambassador to the UK, Dr Pedro Teotónio Pereira was a huge supporter of this idea believing that such a race would bring together the youth of the world's seafaring people. Over the course of three years the two men discussed and formulated their ideas and in 1956 the Tall Ships Race was founded.

In July 1956, twenty ships, with several hundred trainees from ten countries on board, lined up off Torbay on the South West Coast of England for the start of the inaugural Tall Ships Race to Lisbon in Portugal.

The fleet of ships lining up at the start of the first race in 1956 from Torbay

The winner of the overall race was the British ship Moyana. However, disaster struck when she was on her way back to the UK, and she broke up in a bad storm. Luckily all 23 people on board were safely rescued.

The Moyana before she was shipwrecked. All her crew were saved

The Race was intended as a one-off event but it received so much international publicity, that Sail Training International; the group set up to run the race; decided to do it again.. and again, therefore in July 2018 the Tall Ships Races will celebrate their 62nd year.

The annual event takes place in European waters over the summer months. It consists of two racing legs of several hundred nautical miles, and a "cruise in company" between the legs. Over fifty-percent of the crew of each ship participating in the races must consist of young people between the ages of 15-25 years old.

Although it's called the Tall Ships Race, a tall ship does not actually describe a specific type of sailing vessel, but rather a monohulled sailing vessel of at least 9.4 metres (30 ft) that must be conducting sail training and education under sail voyages. Participating ships range from smaller yachts in the Class C/D categories up to the Class A large square-rigged sail training ships run by charities, schools and navies of other countries.

In 2007, The Tall Ships Races were nominated for the Nobel Peace Prize. Norwegian MP Svein Roald Hansen, who put them forward, said *"The vision they share, exemplified by the traditions and achievements of their international events and other activities, demonstrate such a strong coherence with the ethos of the Peace Prize."*

Today, the Races can attract a diverse fleet of international vessels from up to 30 different countries with over 10,000 trainees. And, they can bring up to five million visitors and 400 media representatives to the ports they visit.

The Voyage of a Lifetime

When I received a letter telling me that I had been successful in my application to be a crew member on the Tall Ships Race, it was the beginning of a new chapter of my life and one which truly shaped the person I have become today.

Boarding the TS Sir Winston Churchill in Sunderland in July 1993 I had no idea what the next three weeks held in store for me. I was nervous yet very excited to take on this unknown challenge and threw myself into every task with as much enthusiasm as I could!

I had no idea if I would suffer from seasickness, get homesick or any other kind of sickness but as my fellow crewmates and I clambered on board with our rucksacks and sleeping bags there was an air of real anticipation at what was to come.

Thirty-nine of us were to share a living space which comprised of triple fold up bunks, two shower rooms with 6 'heads' and a communal table in the middle.

We were separated into three 'watches' of twelve people called the Fore, the Main and the Mizzen (based on the three masts). Each watch had a watch leader; an experienced trainee who had participated in previous tall ships voyages.

Before the ship even left the dock we were taken through a number of safety briefings, including how to put on our life jackets (which needed to be worn at all times apart from when you were sleeping), climbing the rigging whilst attaching our harnesses and a fire drill, where we had to crawl through the corridors below deck blindfolded.

As we passed by Roker pier the 'sail training' began. Hoisting sails, pulling ropes, making knots of every kind, navigating, steering, working together as a team. We had two days of training out in the North Sea and got to experience the 'four hour on four hour off' watches. Normal sleep patterns were disrupted as we settled into living the life of a sailor.

On Tuesday 13th July 1993 (which just so happened to be my birthday) as the sun set in the West, we headed up the River Tyne to be welcomed by hundreds of people. In amongst them were my proud Mum and Dad waving and cheering along with everyone else holding a huge bouquet of flowers.

The next four days were spent berthed on Newcastle Quayside at Spillers Wharf where we were treated like celebrities and I got my first real experience of being one of the tall ships family!

Little did I know the next three weeks would change my life forever and my heart would soon belong to the Tall Ships.

18 May 1992

TYNESIDE
TYNESIDE TEC LIMITED

Dear Naomi

TALL SHIPS NEWCASTLE 1993 YEAR OF MARITIME DISCOVERY

I am delighted to inform you that your application to become a crew member on the Tall Ships Race 1993 has been successful.

As explained at the interview, the TEC will be organising a get together of all the successful candidates here at the TEC for a photo-call and publicity launch.

I will be contacting you in the near future to confirm arrangements.

Once again, well done and I look forward to seeing you and working with you in what I am sure will be a fascinating Year of Maritime Discovery.

Yours sincerely

Paul Lund

PAUL LUND
Tyneside TEC Tall Ships 1993 Co-ordinator

Registered Office: Moongate House, 5th Avenue Business Park, Team Valley, Gateshead, Tyne & Wear NE11 0HF.
Registered No. 2409009 England

SAILING

is a way of life...

...one of the...

FINEST

of lives.

- Carleton Mitchell

Crew members of the Sir Winston Churchill learning how to climb the rigging at the start of the 1993 Tall Ships Race.

A Royal Visit

Over the four days we were berthed on Newcastle Quayside I found it strange to be ogled like an animal in a zoo; everyone wanted to look at the ships and watch what the crew were doing. The craziest day was when Prince Edward came on board to visit the crew of the Sir Winston Churchill and the Malcolm Miller. I was one of four trainees lucky enough to have my name picked out of a hat to meet him in person.

When he came up to me and shook my hand I was just in awe that I was meeting a member of the Royal family - the son of the Queen no less. So, when he asked me where I came from I could have kicked myself when I blurted out 'Er, just up the road'!

We couldn't move through the crowds without people stopping us and asking us for our autographs; small children would be thrilled to have their picture taken with us and some would even tell us that they wanted to be a sailor when they grew up. It was an amazing experience.

Our time on the Quayside came to an end with the most amazing crew parade through the city. The Parade is intended to thank the host port for their hospitality and everyone lines the streets and joins in with the festivities. It's a real party atmosphere with most crews wearing fancy dress and carrying flags.

The Crew Parade concludes with a Prize-giving Ceremony in the city centre with prizes being awarded to ships and individuals for a range of disciplines and achievements.

Aside from the serious prizes of which ship won the race in each class, there are also prizes given out for being 'The Best in Crew Parade' or 'Most fun crew'; however, the most coveted prize is the Sail Training International Friendship Trophy. This prize stems from Bernard Morgan's original ambitions and is awarded to the ship which has done more than any other to promote international relations and friendship over the course of the Race.

No one knows who will win this trophy until it is announced as the Captains and permanent crew of all of the competing vessels select the winner by a secret ballot. Every ship wants to win this prize!

July 1993
Crowds are gathered on Newcastle Quayside as Prince Edward boards the
Sir Winston Churchill to meet the crew and the sail trainees.

Tall ships ahoy!

All hands on deck! The TEC crew practise their ropework
on board ship

Twelve young people from Tyneside will be riding the crest of a wave next year thanks to the TEC.

They are being sponsored by the TEC to take part in the 1993 Tall Ships Race from Newcastle to Bergen in Norway.

Two of the ships, the Sir Winston Churchill and the Malcolm Miller, will be crewed mainly by local people.

Tyneside TEC is to cover all the costs for those it has sponsored.

The 12 youngsters are: Julie Bloxham of Benwell; Joanne Lowther, North Shields; Paula Trewick, Whitburn; Clare Hines, Jarrow; Craig Beaty, Fenham; Cameron Train and Jason Spiller, both South Shields; Naomi Austin, Benton; Ivan Whittaker, Throckley; Michael Blevins, Hebburn; Angela Templeton, Gateshead; and Louise Wentworth of North Shields.

One of the youngsters, Clare Hines, aged 21, said: "I was delighted to hear that the TEC was sponsoring me in the Tall Ships Race. I see this as an opportunity to make new friends and enjoy myself, but also an opportunity to learn new skills, especially about how to work together as a team."

Explaining why the TEC has lent its support to the race, chief executive Olivia Grant said: "Tyneside TEC is keen to foster the spirit of enterprise and endeavour among young people. The experience of taking part in the race will build confidence and character and illustrate the importance of teamwork – all crucial attributes in today's business environment.

"We are also pleased to help organise training at South Tyneside College for all those taking part. Doing so clearly demonstrates our commitment to the event and the importance of training to young people. We also firmly believe in the future of Tyneside and maintain a strong desire to ensure it becomes an even better place to live and work in."

In addition to sponsoring the 12 young people, the TEC has also agreed to organise the programme of training for the 100 people being recruited for the Year of Maritime Discovery, of whom 78 will be selected to take part in the race.

The Year of Maritime Discovery has been devised by the Tyne and Wear Development Corporation in conjunction with the TEC and the Northumbria STA Schooners Committee. The recruits will explore the seafaring history of Tyne and Wear with visits to maritime centres and tuition in sea and sailing skills.

One of the many newspaper articles the chosen twelve lucky trainees (including me) featured in.

179

Behold the threaden...

SAILS

...borne with the invisible and creeping...

WIND

...draw the huge bottoms through
the furrow'd...

SEA

...breasting the lofty surge.

- William Shakespeare

Never a...

SHIP

...sails out of the bay,

but carries my...

HEART

...as a stowaway

- Roselle Mercier Montgomery

The view of the deck of the Sir Winston Churchill taken whilst I was sat on the bowsprit.

Seasickness

Sea sickness is one of the biggest fears of a first-time sail trainee - or even an experienced sailor! It's usually caused by the rocking motion of the boat on the water and affects the individual's inner ear as it is the area of the body that affects your overall sense of balance and equilibrium.

I was so lucky in that I didn't experience sea sickness at all which was so strange as I suffer badly from car sickness. However, my crew mates weren't so lucky and about fifteen of them spent the first few days of training lying utterly exhausted on the deck.

Tips to overcome sea sickness:

Spend as much time as possible out on the deck. When you are outside you can look at the horizon, and watching the horizon allows your body to maintain its equilibrium.

If you're on a large ship, staying in the middle of it can make a big difference in combating those rocking and rolling feelings. The middle of the ship is also a natural balance point. If you have a window in your room, it will also let you keep a steady eye on the horizon outside without needing to be on deck.

The bigger the ship, the smoother the ride! It's absolutely true: a choppy sea will feel much bumpier in a smaller boat than it would in a large one.

If you have tried these ideas in the past and they haven't helped much, you can also pick up an over the counter anti-sickness remedy, or try a natural remedy, such as ginger. Children are the most susceptible to seasickness, so it is always a good idea to bring something along, just in case!

Sleeping off the seasickness on the triple bunks aboard the Churchill.

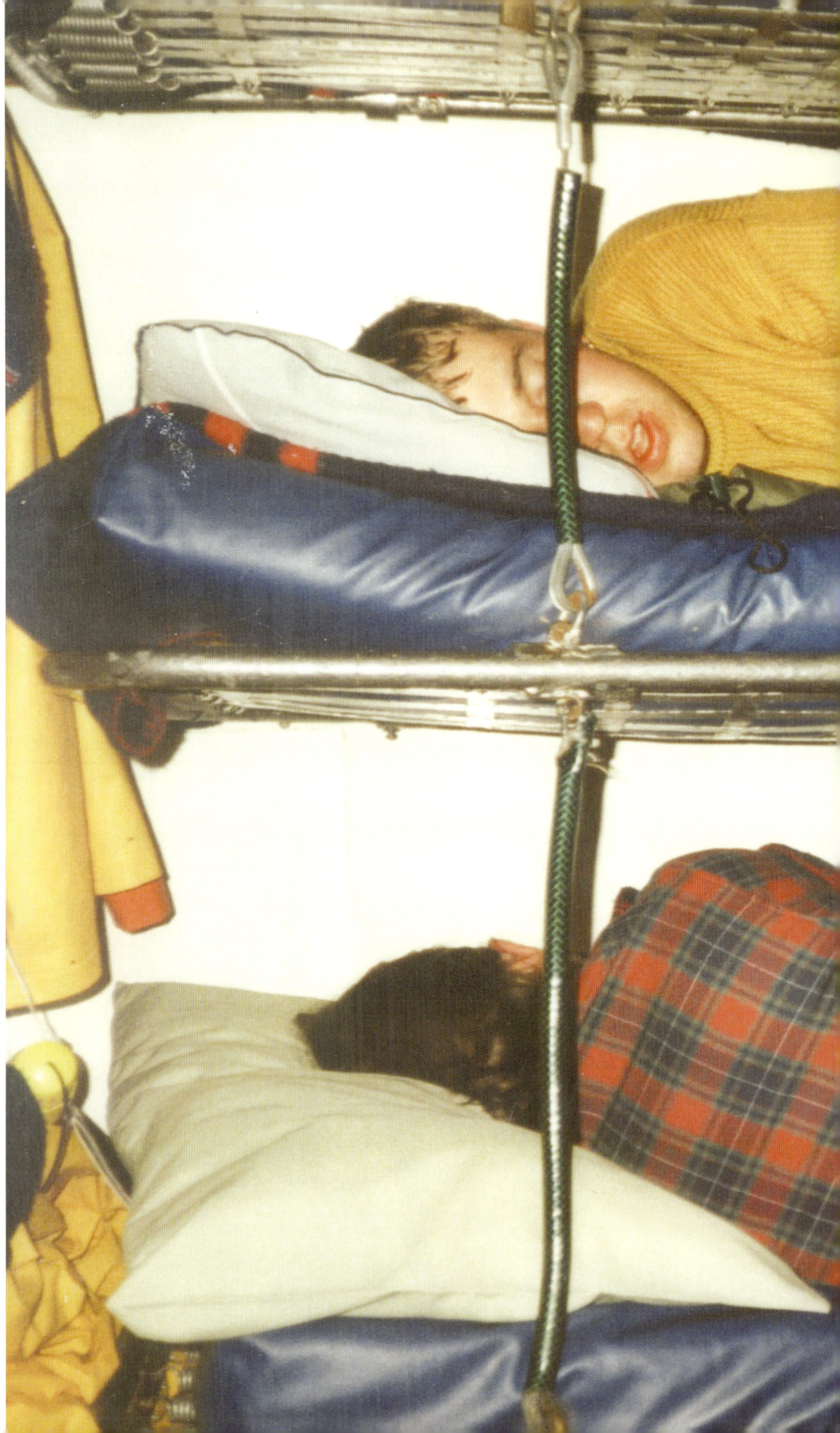

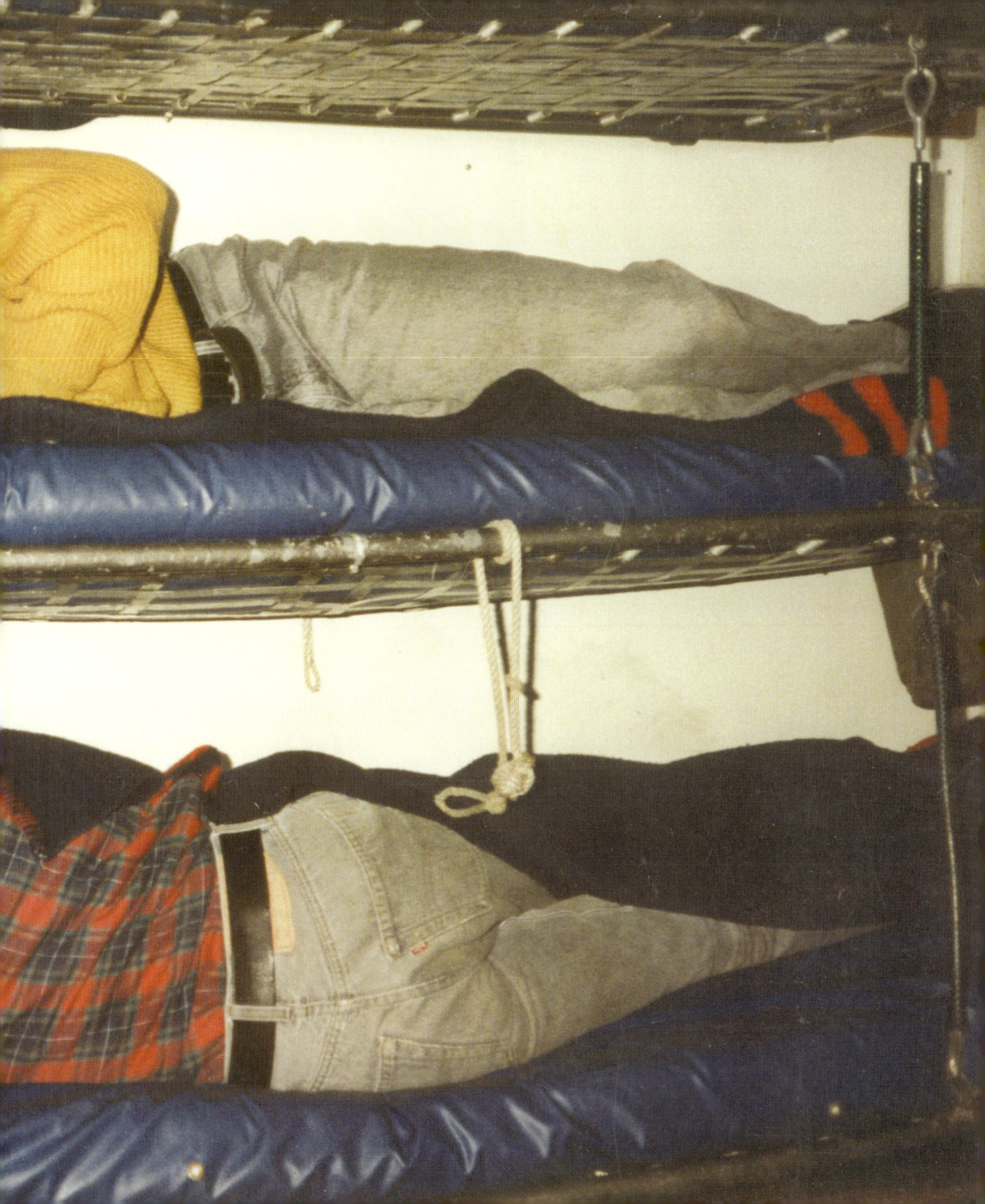

Fair winds and Following Seas

On Saturday 17th July 1993 we finally left Newcastle Quayside to head down the Tyne towards the North Sea and our voyage across to Norway.

As the ship was manoeuvered into position I was given the go ahead to climb the yard arms. I attached my harness and clung onto my disposable camera for dear life as the crowds cheered below and I was able to look back towards the Tyne Bridge and what is now the Baltic Art Gallery. Behind us was the STS Malcolm Miller, the Churchill's sister ship with her trainees mirroring our positions.

As we headed out past Tynemouth Priory and South Shields lighthouse I was overcome with just how many people had turned up to see us off. It was a beautiful day and there wasn't a patch of grass left visible on the riverside with people filling every available vantage point.

We then took part in the 'Parade of Sail'. This is a spectacular line up of the whole fleet, most in full sail before the race is started. It's a breathtaking and unforgettable sight!

I had no idea what was ahead of me apart from the North Sea and all it had to throw at us but when this photo was taken I was ready to take on whatever challenges I faced.

13th July 1993
My birthday was spent in the middle of the North Sea with just my fellow crewmates, one party popper and a crust of bread with some candles which refused to light in the wind!

The STS Sir Winston Churchill in the foreground and her sister ship, the STS Malcolm Miller behind.

Picture credit:
Photo montage - Colin Sanger 1993
photo of Winston Churchill: Max Mudie

Holding on to the top yard arm with my fellow trainee Martin as we came into Bergen harbour after crossing the North Sea.

THE SAIL TRAINING ASSOCIATION
Registered as a Charity

Patron: His Royal Highness The Prince Philip, Duke of Edinburgh, K.G.

STA

The track chart for voyage C482 from Newcastle to Bergen July 1993

VOYAGE: C.482

11TH JULY – 24TH JULY 1993

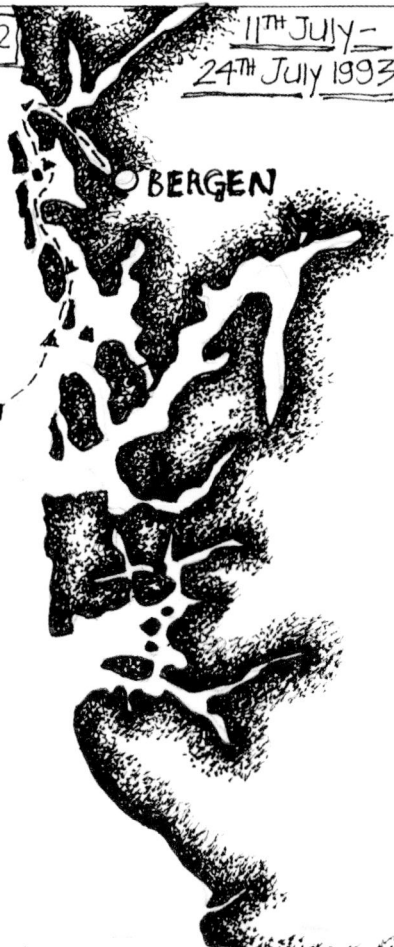

○ BERGEN

I'M NOT ONE TO GOSSIP.... BUT !!!

WIND DECIDED TO TAKE A BREAK!..

PIT STOP AT ESSO OIL RIGS FOR SWEETIES, CANS & 5,000 LION TOKENS

BUT WHAT TIME IS 6PM ?!*

AVERAGE SPEED: 4·67 KNOTS
TOTAL DISTANCE: 669 MILE
UNDER SAIL: 530·2
MOTOR/SAIL: 43·6
MOTOR: 95·2

"THE LOVEY DUCKS FROM THE LURVE BOAT"

Permanent crew
& Afterguard :–
Captain: M. Forwood
Mate: H. O'Neill
Navigator: A. Wilson
Engineer: M. Stephens
Bosun: G. Thorpe
Cook: J. Froggatt
Bosun's mate: M. Hopper
Cooks asst.: A. Jeffrey
Purser: C. Simpson
S/Numerary: G. Westwood

VISIT TO HARRY RAMSDEN'S-N/CLE

THE CUTTY SARK
TALL SHIPS
RACE 1993

Fore Watch:	Main Watch	Mizzen Watch
W.O Bill Smith	W.O Marcel Kortekaas	W.O: Jim Moyes
W.L Ian Stewart	W.L Iain Riddick	W.L: Liz Mawson
1: Mary Askew	1: Louise Whitworth	1: Clare Hines
2: Julie Bloxham	2: Johanne Ramshaw	2: Naomi Austin
3: Craig Beaty	3: Helen Brindley	3: Steve Collins
4: Louise Dinnington	4: James Elliott	4: Jane Forster
5: Andrea Gilbertson	5: Darren Grant	5: Anthony Hackney
6: Gillian Henderson	6: Anna Hemmiker	6: Sarah Hewison
7: Ivan Whittaker	7: Christopher Hinder	7: Joanne Lowther
8: Peter Manghan	8: Julie Maven	8: Mark McLaughlin
9: Gary Morgan	9: Xena Morrison	9: Julie O'Neill
10: Timothy Ogden	10: Paul Oliver	10: Jason Orchard
11: John Palliser	11: Graeme Proud	11: Michael Reed
12: Ahmedur Reznan	12: Emma Robinson	12: Martin Sancaster
13: Susan Taws	13: Jason Spiller	12: Brian Welsh

NEWCASTLE
UPON TYNE
SUNDERLAND

Heading up the Tyne on the evening of Tuesday
13th July 1993, after three days of sail training.

My view from the top yard arm of
the Sir Winston Churchill whilst we
headed down the River Tyne to
start the Tall Ships Race 1993

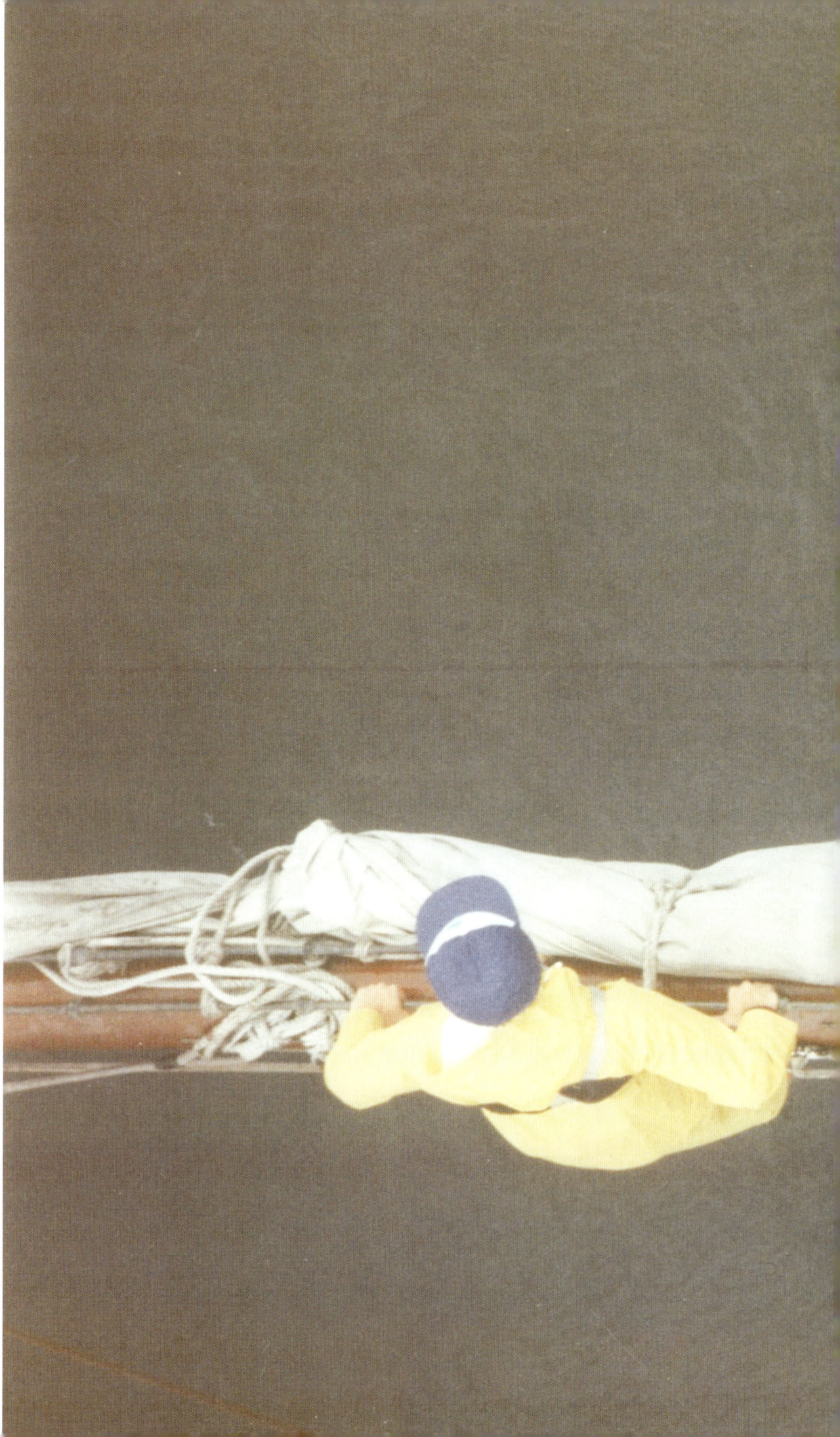

3 ships tied up in Bergen port -
The Sir Winston Churchill and the
Malcolm Miller from the UK and
the Johann Smidt from Germany.

SIR WINSTON CHURCHILL

Owners: Sail Training Association. Built: R. Dunston Ltd, Hessle. Design: Camper & Nicholson. Rig: Top Sail Schooner. Launched: 1966. Tons: Gross 218·6, Net 31

This poster hangs pride of place in my hallway. It was given to every sail trainee at the end of our tall ships voyage. The mission was to get as many of your fellow crewmates to sign it. I think I did quite well.

Running a Tight Ship

My experience of being a sail trainee on the Tall Ships Race in 1993 was one of the greatest things I've done to this day. It gave me the confidence to take on any challenge thrown at me and instilled a real belief that teamwork is the most important element of running not just a ship, but a business or event.

In his online article 'Four Leadership Rules of Sailing' (*www.aboutleaders.com/four-leadership-rules-of-sailing Nov 21st 2017*), David McCuistion explains that one of his sailing instructors; a retired Navy Captain, said there are four rules of sailing which can be followed when developing any leadership skills:

Keep the people in the boat - or on the team
Take care of your people. Ensure that their basic physiological needs are being met. Maintain a safe and secure work environment, treat everyone with respect and dignity, create an environment of empowerment and creativity to build confidence and self-esteem, and permit them to grow emotionally, spiritually and morally in a way that gives meaning and purpose to their lives. In short, a leader values each team member as someone who keeps the boat sailing toward its intended objective, and the overall mission for success.

Keep the water out of the boat - protect them
Prevent contradictory leadership from sources that disrupt the team and question the motive and legitimacy of the leader. Support them, take steps to build team-member confidence and trust that says, "I trust that you made the right decision and that you are working for the good of the team."

Don't hit anyone - Conflict Resolution
Leadership must be ready and capable to resolve conflicts, regardless of the magnitude of the problem. Leaders need to be skilled in relationship building with empathy, exhibiting a caring attitude about individual success and professional growth.

You have to look good - Professional Appearance
External perception is extremely important to the success of the overall team.
Looking good means your professional appearance is sharp, neat, and clean. Team appearance projects a professional customer service attitude that enhances the team abilities to meet the needs of the customer.

We often use the phrase, *'All hands on deck'* and this, of course is a nautical term; an order for all crew members to be available to assist with an activity or event. So, in our everyday lives we need to be adaptable, to *'take on board'* new ideas and be open to suggestions. We could all learn so much from sailing a ship.

STA

This is to Certify that

Naomi Austin

sailed as a member of the crew of

S.T.S. SIR WINSTON CHURCHILL

on voyage C482

from July 11 19 93 to July 24 19 93

MJYorwood

Master

...all your...

DREAMS

...are on their way...

...see how they shine, oh, if you need a friend I'm...

SAILING

...right behind.

- Paul Simon

Some of the crew of the Malcolm Miller watching the awards presentation at the end of the crew parade in Szczecin, Poland during the 2017 Tall Ships Race.

In 2010 I was a volunteer Ship Liaison Officer for the 2nd time responsible for looking after the crew and trainees of the TS Pelican of London whilst they were based in Hartlepool. I got to know Ben Swain who was First Officer at the time but 8 years on he has moved onwards and very much upwards.

Tell me a bit about yourself:

"I am currently Captain on board the TS John Jerwood (a power training vessel) and the Sea Cadet Training Ship's TS Royalist (a Sail Training Brig) both especially designed and built to facilitate to our cadets the skills of navigation, seamanship and teamwork (with a strong essence of adventure!). The Sea Cadets is a national youth organisation run by the Marine Society with close association to the British Royal Navy. It has units all around the country which organise a whole range of activities for young people aged 12-18 to get involved one of which is spending time offshore with me!"

How did you get involved in sailing on a Tall Ship?:

"I was first introduced into Sailing by my stepfather who had an active role in converting the TS Astrid with Cdr Graham Neilson who also built the TS Pelican of London. I was 17 and I hated it at first, thought it was a dreadful experience. I was really sea sick and could not wait to get off but as soon as I did I wanted to go back and do it again.

Then after I recovered from breaking my back I was sponsored to go on the Astrid again, this time on a 3-month voyage across the Atlantic Ocean. The voyage changed my life, really developed my confidence and huge self-esteem, I was hooked, and found myself sailing on tall ships nearly every holiday. I even tried to hold down a "proper job" as Station Manager of Kings Cross Station in London, but the sea came calling for me, and I now get paid to do a job I absolutely love doing. Working with young people in sail training is so rewarding."

Which ships have you sailed on?

"Have you enough room for my list?! The Astrid, Sir Winston Churchill, Malcom Miller, Lord Nelson, Tenacious, and the Stavros Niarchos, Prince William, Maybe, Lady of Avenel, Provident, Royalist (old and New) and that's the ones I remember."

What is the best thing about participating in a Tall Ships Race?

"Where do you begin?! I love everything about the races, the gathering of the fleet, the excitement of the ships, the colour of the flags, the mix of cultures of the crews from different countries, the sailing, the talks of race tactics, the tales of waypoints missed. Fundamentally though, it is the wealth of international friendships I have gained, from Sweden to Oman, Japan to Canada, friendships formed across oceans, knotted together by shared adventure that have tested the winds of time. My life is enriched as a result. I also love the crew parades, when I get to dress up as a pirate!"

The original TS Royalist passing the docks of the
River Tyne heading out to the North Sea to take
part in the first leg of the 1993 Tall Ships Race.

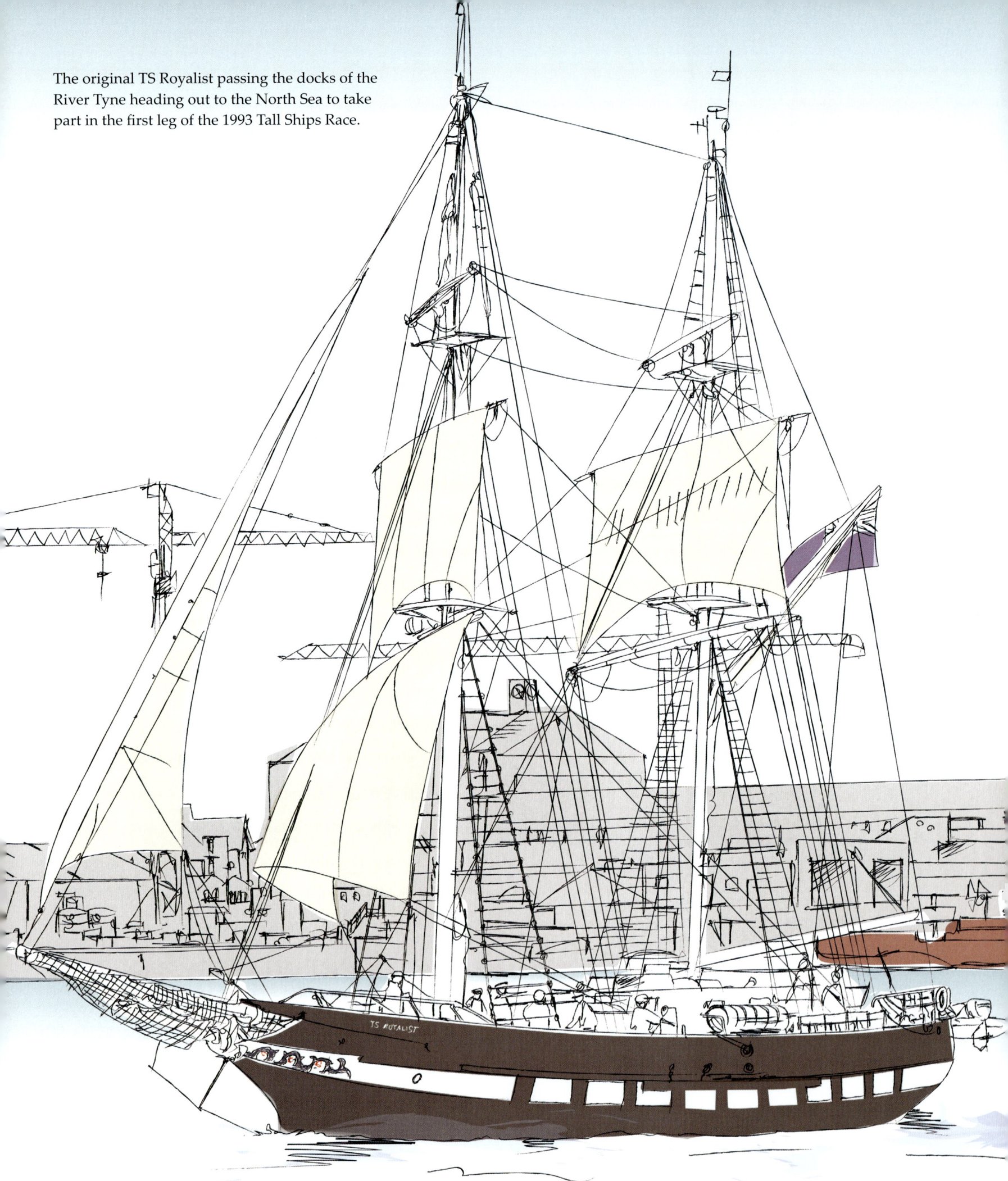

What is the best thing about sailing on a Tall Ship?

The blue sky, the sunsets, the smell of the wind, but the greatest thing is the way it brings people of different backgrounds, regions, countries, and different cultures, able-bodied and disabled, young and old into one unified team. A ship cannot be sailed by an individual but an enthusiastic ships company that share a collection of unique amazing moments on every voyage.

What is the most challenging thing?

Tall ships sailing has many challenges, and each individual to the person experiencing them, the greatest challenge using all the personal achievements, and personal development and not becoming addicted to wanting to keep discovering more. But that's not a bad thing!

Where have you sailed to on a Tall ship?

"I have been so lucky; I have sailed in the Caribbean, Central America, the Baltic, the Mediterranean, and the West Coast of Africa, and all round the UK and Northern Europe, and there are still so many places I want to go.

What is the best memory you have of being part of a Tall Ships Crew?

"I have to name one? Really?! Ok... the most special moment is when I was Bosun on the JST's Tenacious and I shared a sunset aloft with 3 of the amazing disabled crew she carries on board. We had just completed the assisted climbs; there was myself, a lady with cerebral palsy, an injured gulf war veteran, and a blind girl called Amy. For all of them it was a tremendous effort of personal will and determination to achieve each one encouraging the other to get to be sitting on the tops (the 1st platform) and I was just about to broach the subject of descending when Amy asked me to describe the scene. Each one of us took turns to describe what we saw, and I will never forget how Amy looked in the directions we described. It was her final comment that brought us to tears... " I have a picture now and this will form the best memory of my life as I have seen the best sunset in the company of my shipmates. I never thought I could do that", and that is what Tall Ships is all about, forming memories, with friends, and remembering what we can achieve."

Do you have any advice for a wannabe Tall Ships sail trainee who has never done it before?

"Do it, raise the funds and, to use Mark Twain's famous quote.. 'Explore, Sail, Dream and Discover' who you really are'!"

The Captain of the Dar Młodzieży, Ireneusz "Eric' Lewandowski & I during the 2016 Blyth Tall Ships Regatta.
Although Eric was a strict Captain he was also a lot of fun & had a great sense of humour!

After being a Ship Liaison Officer (SLO) for the 2nd time in Hartlepool in 2010 I was thrilled to find out that Blyth, on the coast of Northumberland, had been chosen as one of the host ports for the Tall Ships Regatta in 2016. Immediately I signed up to volunteer again. The Tall Ships Regattas are slightly smaller than the Races with fewer ships but are just as popular with the general public.

Once Europe's busiest coal port, Blyth had struggled in the past. In the 1990s it was dubbed the drugs capital of the UK; however, this problem was tackled very successfully with investment in drugs treatment and counselling as well as huge regeneration projects throughout the area.

Almost 30 years on, the quiet seaside town welcomed around half a million people to the Regatta over the Bank Holiday weekend in August 2016 bringing in millions of pounds to the local economy.

I was SLO for the biggest ship there, the Dar Młodzieży and got to know the crew and trainees over the four days they were in Blyth. It was wonderful to see all the community come together and celebrate the visit of these wonderful ships.

Sailors, with their built in sense of...

ORDER

...service and discipline,

should really be running the...

WORLD

- Nicholas Monsarrat

Four hoarse blasts of a ship's...

WHISTLE

*...still raise the hair on my neck,
and set my feet to...*

TAPPING

— John Steinbeck

To reach a port we must set...

SAIL

...sail, not tie at...

ANCHOR

...sail, not drift

- Franklin D. Roosevelt

Whilst conducting research for this book I came across the amazing photography of Eugenia Romanenko; official photographer for the Russian Tall ship, 'Kruzenshtern'. At first I wanted to just draw from her photos but I felt that her images were too spectacular not to share.

Over a number of months, we have built up a wonderful online friendship and I hope one day I will get to sail with Eugenia on the Kruzenshtern.

Here she tells us a little bit about how she got involved photographing the crew of the second biggest Tall ship in the World.

"I resigned from a stable office job with a large telecommunications company in Russia to work as a steward on the Kruzenshtern. I moved to another city and undertook a degree in photography so when I returned to the ship I was armed with a camera and the intuition that nothing would remain the same.

When people ask me why I became a photojournalist and why am I so interested in the sea and sailing my answer is 'because of the Kruzenshtern; this ship has really changed my whole life.'
But when I'm asked 'why the Kruzenshtern?' I'm not really sure how to answer that - maybe it wasn't me who chose this ship, perhaps the Kruzenshtern chose me!

Of course, the sight of other ships in full sail also excites me and I have other ideas and projects I'd like to undertake; however, at the moment I am extremely glad to be given the opportunity to work on the Kruzenshtern for at least two to three months of the year.

My soul and camera belong to the Kruzenshtern. It makes me happy to have realised my ambition."

For more information and to see more of Eugenia's pictures please visit:
www.instagram.com/seasailshots

©ERomanenko

A sailor is an...

ARTIST

...whose medium is the wind.

LIVE

...passionately, even if it kills you, because something is going to kill you anyway.

- Webb Chiles - Sailor

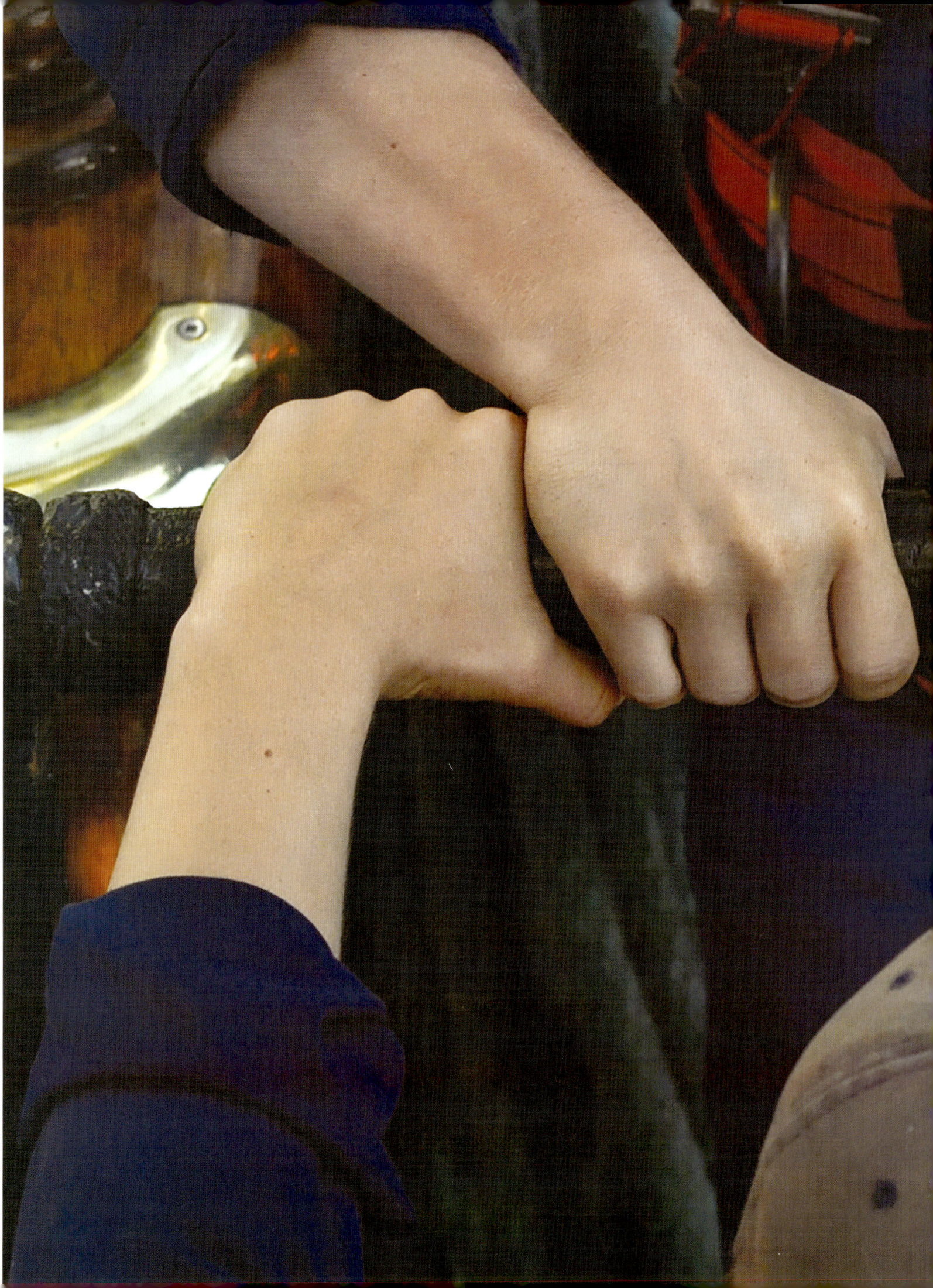

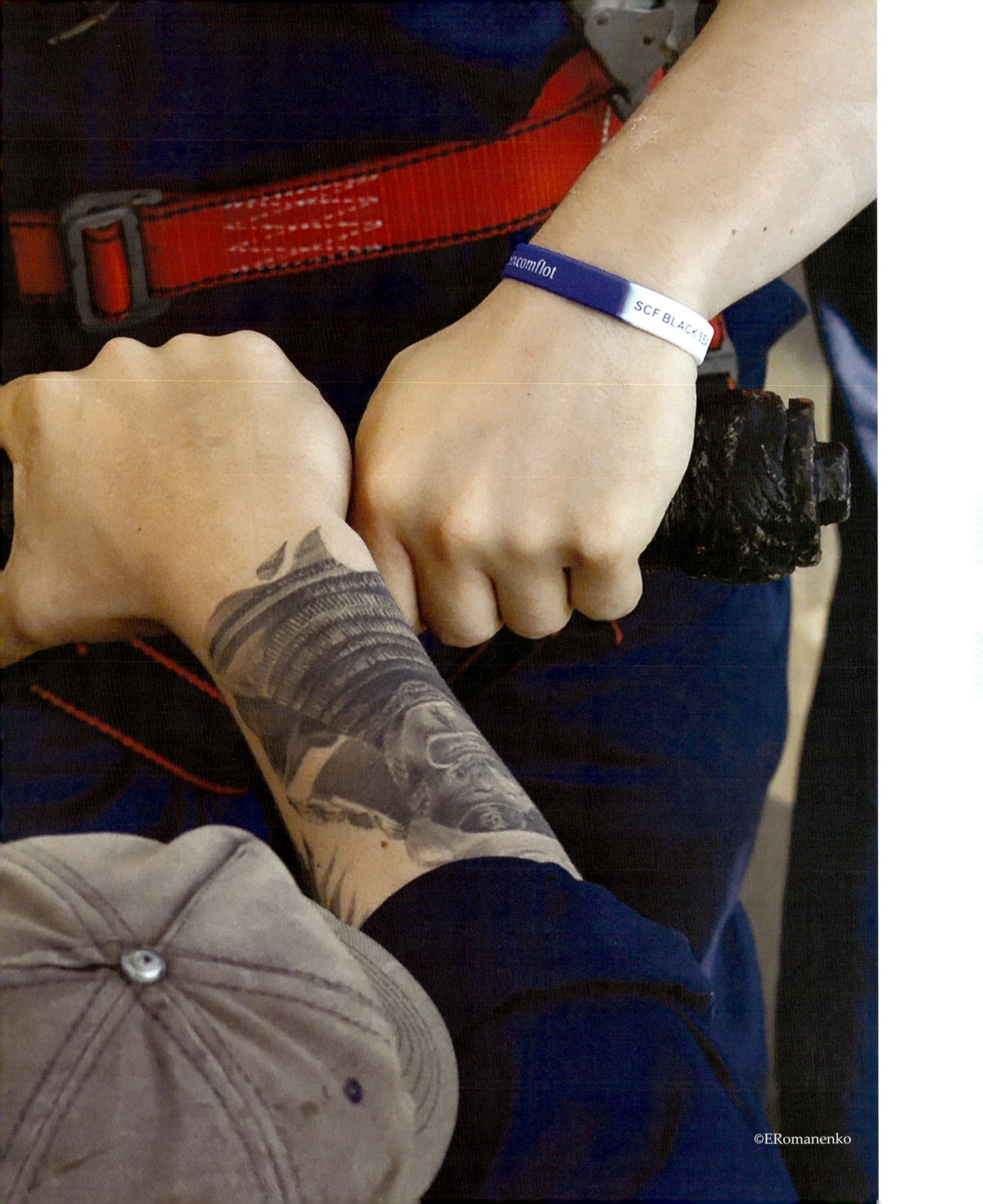

©ERomanenko

©ERomanenko

©ERomanenko

©ERomanenko

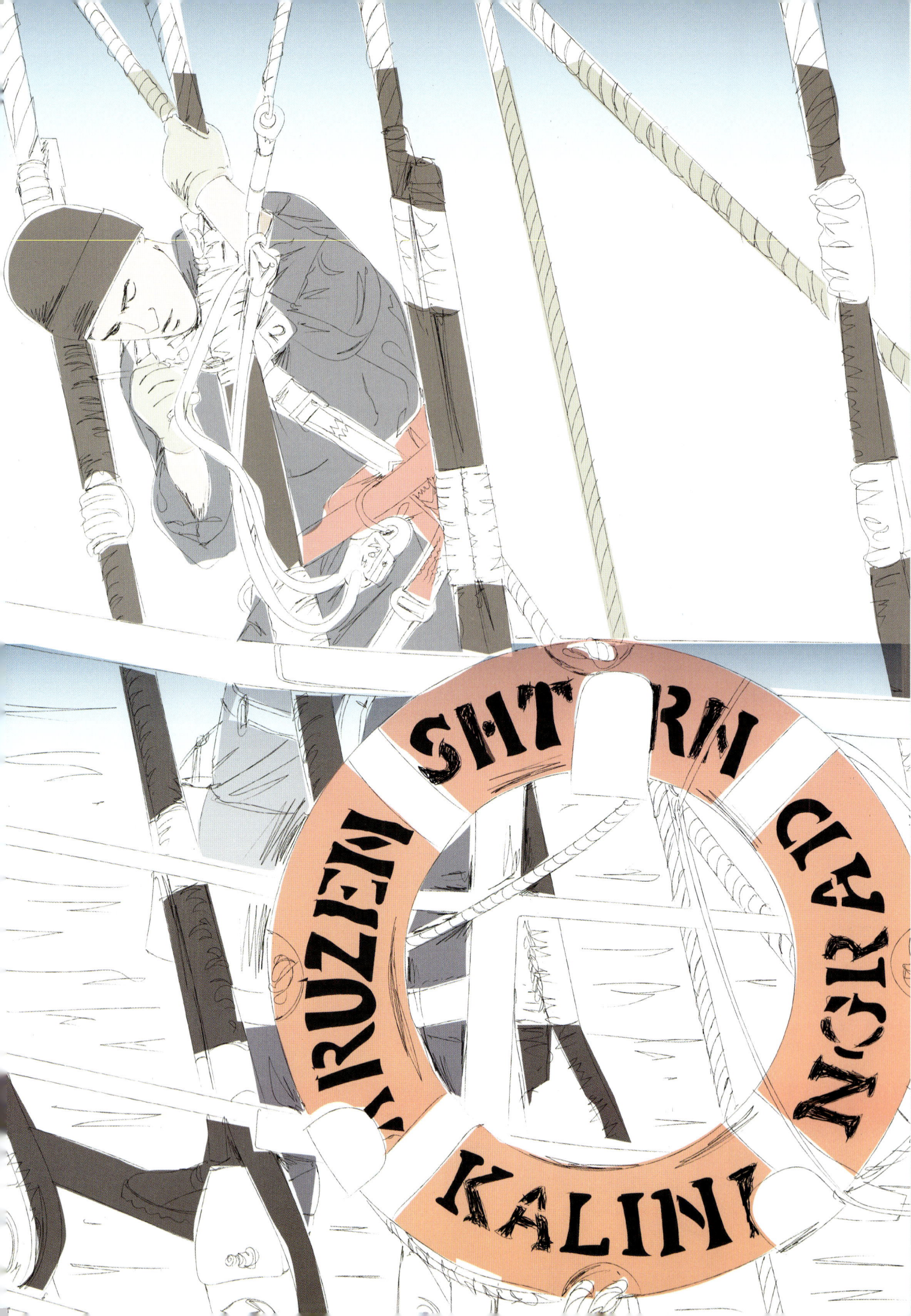

One of the crew of the Kruzenshtern painting
protective coating onto the rigging of the ship.
Maintenance and upkeep of all ships is vital to the
smooth running of it and the crew all participate in
painting, cleaning and renovating every part of it.

©ERomanenko

A panoramic view of the Tall Ships in Szczecin
during the 2017 Race finale.

When I flew to Szczecin in Poland in August 2017 to experience the final of the 2017 Tall Ships Race I was invited to stay aboard the Danish ship Skonnerten Jylland as a guest of Captain Niels Kristensen.

The Skonnerten Jylland (English: Schooner Jutland) is not just any Tall Ship. She was built in 1951 and has been run as a self-governing institution since 2003, first as "Anne el 2" and in 2007 she became the Skonnerten Jylland.

DSI Andromeda was founded on April 1, 2000 by Niels, who started the Andromeda ship project in 1997. The company consists of people on the board. They are self-sufficient and thus elect new members as well as the Board itself which includes a Chairman and Vice-Chairman, etc. The Skonnerten Jylland is the base of the social pedagogical ship project providing a home to a total of six young people who all have their own room on the ship and who live on the ship most of the time. When they are not at sea, the ship is based in Enköping a few miles outside Thisted, Denmark.

Niels and his crew look after, and train, these vulnerable youngsters to live for a period on the ship until they are able to return to society. They often go into education or a new line of work so that they can look after themselves in the future.

Over the years they have worked with many social disadvantaged young people, and young people with ADHD and they've seen amazing results in strengthening the youngster's self-esteem because they develop this through sailing and working together as a team. They teach them responsibility, teamwork and structure to help them to go into adulthood with a stronger sense of being able to meet the increasing demands of society.

They eat and cook together in the galley, and students are taught in the large deck saloon.

The ship participates in several international races, which helps to give the youngsters aboard a life-time experience of teamwork and unity, as well as enhancing their individual self-esteem.
For more information please visit:
www.andromeda.dk

How did you get involved with sailing on a Tall ship?

"My first experience on a tall ship was when I bought the schooner Andromeda in 1997."

Which ship/s have you sailed on and where?

"Since 2010 I have sailed on the Skonnerten Jylland. Usually we sail in Scandinavia, the Baltic and North Sea and I've done trips to Ireland and France."

What is the best thing about sailing on a Tall Ship?

"Friendship and togetherness, and you get to visit new ports and places. I also like the major challenges that come with needing to sail a large ship and the necessity to work 24/7's."

What was/is the best thing about participating in the Tall Ships Race?

"I have sailed in the TSR several times since 2000. I don't remember exactly how many but I think it's about 12-13! The best thing about the TSR is meeting new people and coming across old friends. The social aspect of the TSR is unique; you always feel welcome and nobody is better than anyone else no matter what size ship or type of ship you are sailing on. We are all equal."

Niels Kristensen at the helm of the Skonnerten Jylland in 2017

"What is the best memory you have of being part of a Tall Ships Race Crew?

"It is difficult to designate a single experience as the best. For me, each participation in the TSR is unique and I am looking forward to seeing how the young trainees I have on board develop over the few weeks a TSR takes. I always see young people aboard who are developing completely differently in a positive direction to what they were and I look forward to that every time."

Do you have any advice for a wannabe Tall Ships sail trainee who has never done it before?

"Yes! Just do it and enjoy every moment :-) Always remember to help each other, the ocean is dangerous if you're not working together to sail the ship; be there for your friends and you will develop a bond for life."

The Skonnerten Jylland in the 1970's

The crew of the Danish ship Skonnerten Jylland marching through the city of Szczecin during the Tall Ships Race crew parade. The parades attract thousands of people and are one of the most exciting parts of the whole event with different crews dressing up and vying for the best prizes.

Mike Pedersen is from Denmark and participated in every leg of the 2017 Tall Ships Races at the age of 15.

Tell me about yourself:

"I'm currently at school but I became part of the Skonnerten Jylland 'family' because I was involved in criminal activity. The Danish government paid for me to live on the ship and learn to become a better person. I was on the ship for the whole of my Summer vacation.

The best thing about being part of the Tall Ships Race was meeting so many different people from so many different countries. I loved making new friends.

The most challenging thing was not being able to see my family for a long time.

My favourite memory was being able to take part in the crew parades and parties.

My advice for anyone taking part on a Tall Ships adventure for the first time would be to get to know your fellow crew first. Make friends with them and learn to work together. When you can do that everything will be good."

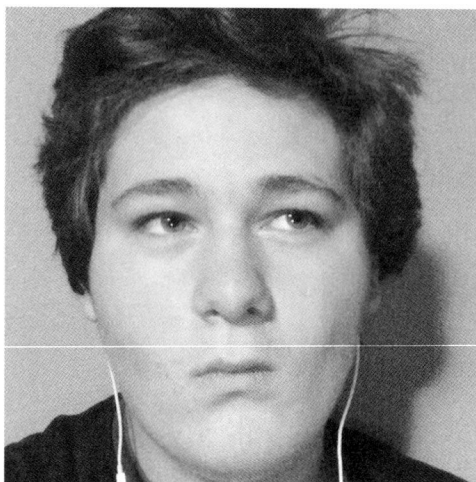

The crew parade through Szczecin Poland - crowds of people came out to cheer the trainees on from their balconies and on the streets.

From left to right: Focus Hotel, Akademia Morska w Szczecinie (Maritime University of Szczecin), Muzeum Narodowe w Szczecinie (The National Museum of Szczecin) and the Kuratorium Oświaty w Szczecinie (Board of Education) as seen from the deck of the Skonnerten Jylland during the Tall Ships Race 2017.

Over the course of putting this book together I managed to contact previous sail trainees, current trainees, Captains, full time crew and even the Tall Ships Race Director from 1976 to 1992; John Hamilton, all who have participated in Tall Ships Races across the years. The following are some of their responses about their personal experiences:

How did you get involved on sailing on a Tall Ship?

"Through school - saw the tall ships leave Liverpool in 1984 wanted to do it!"

"Referred after a Royal Navy interview."

"I saw a TV programme about the STA Schooners in 1972 and decided I wanted to sail - which I did in 1975."

"In 1975 the STA asked for volunteer navigators for their schooners. I was an Army captain but ex MN with 1st Mates ticket so I applied and did my first voyage on Malcolm Miller in June 1975. Many voyages followed in a wide variety of ST vessels."

"When I was 18 I entered a competition in the Nottingham Evening Post. I was offered a fully funded 2-week voyage and 2/3 weeks later I boarded in Blackpool with 4 other girls."

"Brian Stewart of the STA was my boss so, I was volunteered to go on the Malcolm Millar in 1967."

What was the best thing about sailing on a Tall Ship?

"Overcoming the terror, the team work. Finding out I could cope with more than I ever thought."

"Meeting people from different backgrounds, ages and nationalities."

"Going aloft, teamwork, amazing people. Sailing halfway round the world!"

"Personal challenges, working as a team-member, friendships formed."

"I thought then, and still do, that life on a Tall Ship teaches the uninitiated that the Sea is has no respect of personality, station or physical prowess!"

"Working as a team to make a beautiful craft move through the water driven by the wind."

What is the most challenging thing?

"Force 12 winds, climbing up past the crow's nest, going out on the bowsprit in a storm..."

"Going aloft in high winds and letting go to pull the sails in whilst relying on your harness alone! Scary stuff!"
"In my case it was very early in the cruise when I succumbed to seasickness and tried to give in and retire to my bunk, only to be rousted by the Watch Leader and treated by the Master. To my eternal gratitude he put me back on my feet and I never looked back!"

What was the best thing about sailing in a Tall Ships Race?

"Excitement of pushing for max speed."

"Brilliant camaraderie, friendly rivalry between ships, making new friends and catching up with old friends."

"The community feel - feeling part of something much bigger than just our ship."

"Participation and the send-off by hundreds of vessels when leaving Gothenburg. Seeing the Swedish ship in full sail in opposite direction. The flyover by RAF Shackleton middle of North Sea."

What is the best memory you have of being part of a Tall Ships Crew?

"Winning the Cutty Sark Trophy in 1984 with Captain Chris Blake."

"Sat on deck on watch with only a few people awake. It was about 3am; darkness all around. The lights of a tanker disappeared over the horizon and we were alone watching the curvature of the earth on the horizon. Dolphins came alongside. Amazing!"

"Manning the Yards when arriving in Newport Rhode Island in 1976."

"Our watch went to a joke shop in Dieppe. We bought false breasts, fake dog poo and a mouse on a string. We ran the mouse along the table at dinner and freaked out the other watches. We also put the poo on the chartroom floor which freaked out the purser. Everyone was in stitches once they realised what was happening."

Do you have any advice for a wannabe Tall Ships sail trainee who has never done it before?

"Just do it! You won't regret it."

"Stay positive and do your best! Expect to come back a different person :)"

"Participate in as much as you are able. Embrace the opportunity, it's unique and life changing!"

"Be brave, face your fears, and DO IT!"

"Come with a positive attitude and play a full part in being a member of the crew whether it is steering the ship or cleaning the 'heads'. Don't worry if you get sea sick...almost everyone does on their first trip but they soon get over it and that is part of the challenge."

"Leave your preconceptions ashore, and be open to learning, not just from the more experienced, from everyone."

"Go for it. It's the experience of a lifetime!"

Who is the happier man, he who has...

BRAVED

THE STORM

...of life and lived or he

who has stayed securely on...

SHORE

...and merely existed?

- Hunter S Thompson

In late 2017/ early 2018 a number of classes from North East primary schools and students from the University of Sunderland took part in drawing workshops with me.

The primary school children were asked to design a new Tall Ship for Sunderland complete with a flag and uniform and the best ones were chosen from a number of entries. The students from the University were asked to draw an existing Tall ship using mixed media. Over the next few pages are a few examples of the winning entries.

It was fantastic to be involved with these kids and their enthusiasm for the task in hand was heart warming. Thank you to every school and student who took part, particularly Springwell Village Primary School in Gateshead and Valley View Primary School in Jarrow.

Emily Young
Foundation Student at University of Sunderland

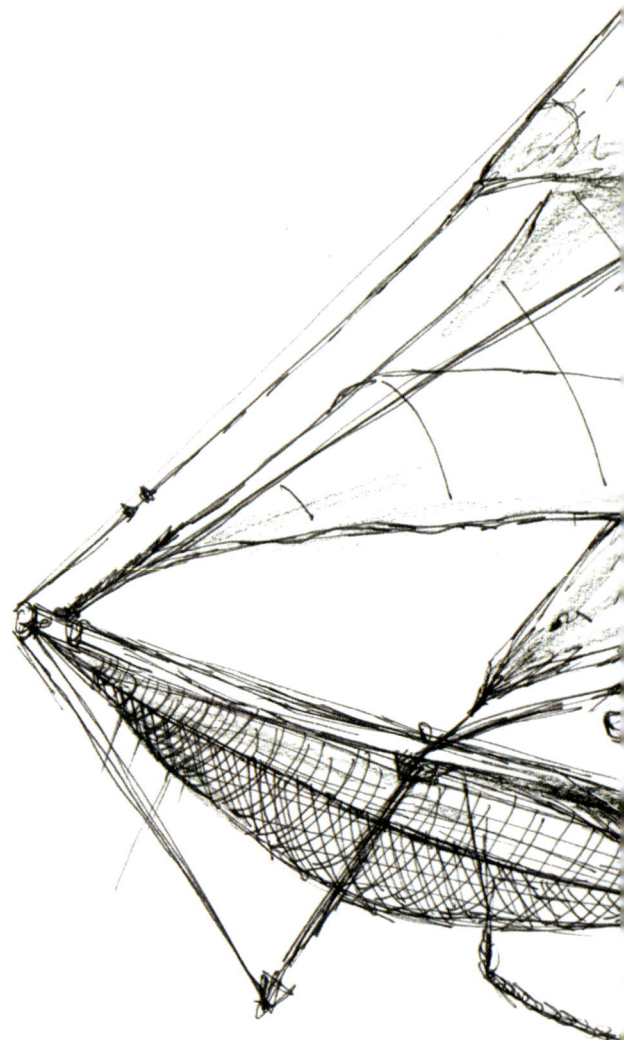

Rachel Scrivens
Foundation Student at University of Sunderland

Lauren Frost
BA Hons Glass & Ceramics
Student at
University of Sunderland

Natalie Martin
BA Hons Fine Art Student at
University of Sunderland

Shaun Mills
BA Hons Fashion Product & Promotion
Student at
University of Sunderland

1st place
George Lavery
Aged 9
Springwell Junior School

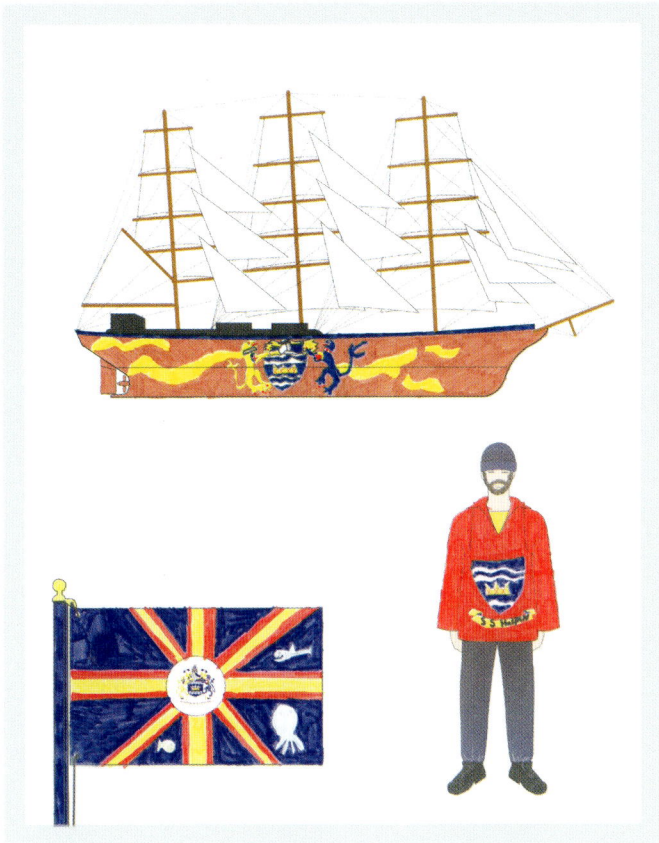

2nd place
Leni May Wilson
Aged 9
Springwell Junior School

3rd place
Gabriel Halpin
Aged 9
Springwell Junior School

Highly commended
Evie Brooke-Lovell
Aged 9
Springwell Junior School

'Explore, Dream, Discover'

A lot has happened over the past 25 years of my life, jobs have changed, locations have changed but one thing that has stayed the same is my love for everything to do with the Tall Ships and what they can do for the self esteem of young people across the World. As a shy child who was bullied at school, going on the Tall Ships Race changed my life for the better.

Young people today are in the grip of the digital age where social media can become an obsession and it's a common sight to see kids fixated on their phones. Everything is accessible with the touch of a button. But I think it's vitally important to be able to teach youngsters about what else is out there for them and I wholly believe we need to all encourage the next generation to get out and see the World.

I have tried to use my experiences to enhance my teaching and I encourage as many young people as possible to participate in active adventures. Getting involved in a sail training event gives them the perfect opportunity as they don't have to have previous experience in sailing, all they need is bags of enthusiasm.

So, the next time you hear a young kid say they're bored two weeks into their long summer holidays give them the details of how to become a sail trainee and maybe they'll go on to *'throw off the bowlines, sail away from the safe harbour, explore, dream, discover'* and have the time of their lives!

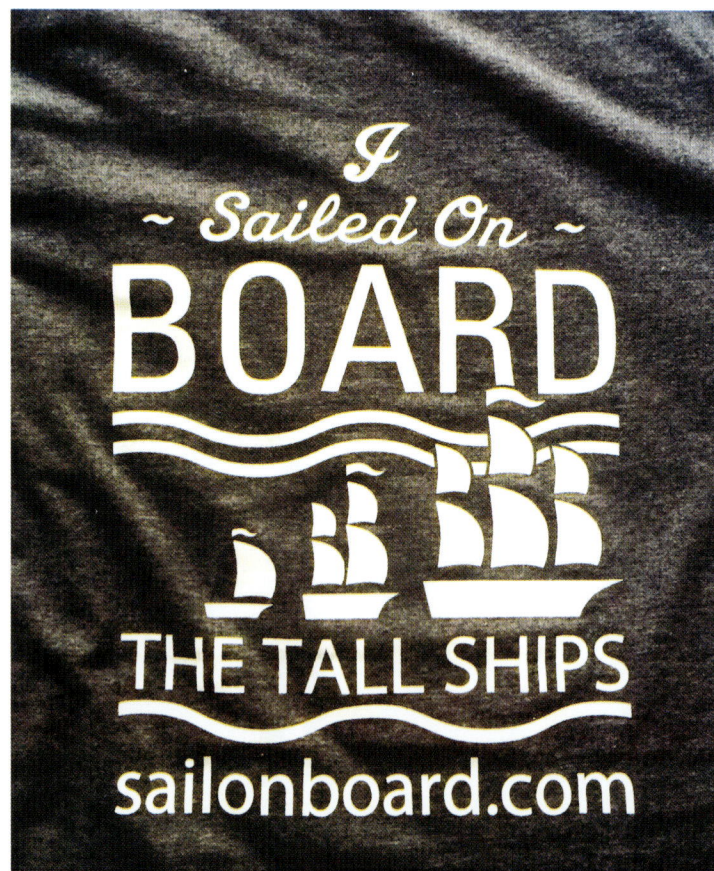

ACKNOWLEDGEMENTS

This book would simply not have been possible without the support and guidance from so many people.

I am completely indebted to the Sunderland Maritime Heritage Museum and their amazing volunteers, in particular Jack Curtis who inspired me from the day we met in Autumn 2017.

For the historical information on shipbuilding on the Wear and their fantastic memories, Alf Redford, Anthony Renton, Meg Hartford, Don Simpson - sincerely, thank you!

The financial support provided by Kate and Stuart Felton gave me the chance to see this idea develop from a dream into reality, for which I am extremely grateful.

It's no exaggeration when I say this book would not have seen the light of day without the encouragement, advice and support of my colleagues from the University of Sunderland - Professor Ewan Clayton, Kathryn Brame and Dr. Mike Collier. Their enthusiasm for, and understanding of, this project has kept me going when at times I felt like giving up.

A special mention must go out to Jill Kirkham, my close colleague and friend who has endured me talking about ships on more or less a daily basis for eight months.

Thank you to my friend Dr. Gareth Evans for casting his eye over the editing and final proof-reading.

And finally, to my amazing family - I heeded your words, I was keen and I did it, I actually did it!

Thanks also go to the following:

George Clarke for writing such a wonderful foreword.

The skippers of the ships, Ben Swain (TS John Jerwood & TS Royalist), Niels Kristensen (Skonnerten Jylland), Ireneusz Lewandowski (Dar Młodzieży) and Calvin Whitehand (Black Diamond of Durham) for having me on board.

To all the past and present sail trainees and Tall Ships crew who replied to me with their individual, remarkable and inspiring memories and stories.

Eugenia Romanenko (Евгения Романенко) for the stunning photographs of the crew of the Kruzenshtern hard at work.For more information please contact her at: er.nautic@gmail.com

Tyne and Wear Archives for providing access to the fantastic photographs of shipbuilding on the River Wear.
For more information please visit: *www.twarchives.org.uk*

Wear Built Ships Database (Shipping & Shipbuilding Research Trust) for helping me to ensure I got my Sunderland ship statistics correct! For more information please visit:
www.sunderlandships.com

Sail Training International for the statistics and facts on the ships currently participating in the Tall Ships Races. For more information please visit: *www.sailonboard.com*

To everyone at Windseeker, particularly Janine and Monique who helped to realise my dream of participating in another Tall Ships Race 25 years after I first took part.
To enquire about adventures on the Tall Ships please visit:
www.windseeker.org

To everyone at UK Book Publishing; particularly Dan and Jay who have believed in me enough to agree to publish this rookie's first book!

Finally I would like to express my great appreciation to the following friends, family and supporters who invested in this book before it even went to print:

Tony Ahlstam
Alan Ainsworth
Graham Brack
Laura Price Charlton
David Copeland
Roy Davis
Liz Headon
Barbara Knight
Adam Marsh
Dave and Lyndsey Pokhan
Derran Sewell
Frances Sewell
Helen and John Simmons
Mark 'Penfold' Simpson
John and Thelma Walker
Gemma Williamson

If there's anyone I've missed, then please accept my apologies but thank you nonetheless!

**Certain information has been adapted from Wikipedia: The Free Online Encyclopedia. The statistics have been verified for authenticity using other online reference material.

"May you always have Fair Winds & Following Seas"